THE

Rib

CONNECTION

SECRETS TO
DEVELOPING
HEALTHY
RELATIONSHIPS

Carlos L. Malone, Sr.

The Rib Connection: Secrets to Developing Healthy Relationships

ISBN: 978-0-924748-83-7
UPC: 88571300053-6

Printed in the United States of America
© 2007 by Carlos L. Malone, Sr.

Milestones International Publishers
140 Danika Dr. NW
Huntsville, AL 35806
(256) 830-0362; Fax (256) 830-9206
www.milestonesintl.com

1 2 3 4 5 6 7 8 9 10 11 / 10 09 08 07

Dedication

———✦———

I want to pay memorable tribute to the two persons who gave me life and substance——they are my parents, Roosevelt Malone, Sr., and Mary Lee Malone. Without the helpful hand and heart of these two persons, there is no Carlos Malone. My parents have both just recently, within the last eighteen months, departed from this life and are now having to watch me from a different seat and view in the arena of eternal life and joy——they are still influencing me to be the best that I can be. I love them both and miss them both more than I can express. My life and legacy will serve as my honorable tribute to them for always giving me the best that they could. Mommy and Daddy, your number-three child really misses you and wishes that you were still here on Earth.

I also pay tribute to Kevin, who is the second oldest of my siblings. He also went home unexpectedly to be with the Lord at the young age of forty-nine, within the same eighteen-month time period as my parents. You were a true brother and a motivator to all of your siblings and to everyone that you met.

Acknowledgements

—————

There is a biblical and yet philosophical principle that I have chosen throughout my life and use as a reminder of how I have been able to make it in and through life's challenges and changes. That principle is the one that says "no man lives to himself." This has always been a yoke of influence that has helped me to have a clear and clarified understanding of the important value of the existence of people who allow you to have entrance into their lives. My life has been influenced by so many people, far too many to even mention and many who I can't remember because I have been exposed to people and their influences on my life ever since I came into this world. However, there are some persons to whom I owe public acknowledgement due to their private place in my life. I do not list these persons in a format of prioritized importance, but rather chronologically and in historical significance.

To the Redeemer of my life and soul, the Lord Jesus Christ who has given me salvation and eternal hope: I reverence you for giving me the gifts and abilities to represent you in all that I do. I hope that I have done you honor in the writing of this document of life strategies that will impart truth into marriages and relationships so that they may remain strengthened and structured after your likeness. I offer you my praise as a tribute of my love.

I have six brothers—— Ricardo, Kevin, Roosevelt Jr., Roderick, Steve, and Jarrod——and three sisters——Veronica, Carmen, and Genyne——all of whom I love very dearly; I am proud to be called their brother. Kevin, I think about you every day and I miss you every day.

On June 21st 1980, I married a pretty young girl named Pamela Renee Barfield. We were both twenty-two years of age with no clue about being married. However, we have been able to sustain our marriage through all of the challenges for twenty-seven years. It is to Pamela that I acknowledge my love and give tribute for the years of experiences that have given me the credibility to be able to pen this book with undeniable integrity. Thanks for the years.

To my most precious possessions, my children Ashley, Andrea, and Carlos Jr.: you give me motivation and determination to excel beyond my own expectations. I challenge you to always strive for excellence without excuse and to maintain a life of character and integrity. Keep God first and you will never come behind in anything. I love you all very much. To my godson Raymond: you are a true source of encouragement to me. Grow forward and go forward into your purpose, for you are loved by me and blessed by God.

To the saints of the Bethel Church of Miami, Florida: thank you for your continual support of my family and me. I hold you high on my list because you have been there through my growing years as a pastor and you continue to allow me to grow through trial and error and you keep showing up in great numbers to be taught by me. My love for you is genuine and forever.

To all of the persons whose names are too many to mention who have in any way supported my life: thanks for your confidence and prayers, for they have carried me and continue to carry me into unimaginable territories and life-changing experiences.

May those who read this book find strength through the struggle, strategies through the stress, and success in your search for love and happiness.

Table of Contents

Preface

————◆————

The visionary purpose behind this book is to provide a resource that will give readers revelation and reality on sensitive subjects that relate to relationships. There is so much powdered and pampered-down information on the shelves of bookstores today that it appears that even when the information is good, it does not always answer or address the questions that people are asking.

When it comes to the real issues of marriage and relationships that people face today, the body of Christ, and even many leaders within the body, often seem to waver and fail to give a clear biblical message. Indeed, Christian believers many times seem to be as confused as everybody else regarding subjects like sex, infidelity, married-but-un-fulfilled, pre-marital sex, divorce, etc. Millions worldwide suffer silently in ignorance and confusion on these issues. And many in the church suffer too.

The body of Christ certainly is not immune. Apart from a divorce rate nearly equal to that of non-believers, consider also the alarming divorce rate of ministry leaders, many of whom in recent years have fallen into the traps of adultery and fornication. This includes some noted pastors and bishops. Many of our religious heroes have succumbed to the fatality of failed ministries because of the hypocrisy of the "super saints" who say it is safer and easier to strip a man or woman of their ministry than to face head-on the infiltration of humanistic philosophies into the hearts and minds of Christians and Christian leaders. These often go unnoticed and unmentioned out of fear of facing the truth or of speaking the truth in a society where truth is considered both relative and irrelevant.

All of us have perplexing issues in our lives that we wish we did not have. Hundreds of books have been written that expose the human frailties and hurts of God's people. I have tried to write a different book, a book that expends medicine and healing to the spirit, mind, and body of all people, and especially Christians.

Truth be told, the people who struggle with their sexuality, troubled marriages, and relationships are not found only in the world, but also within the ranks of those who truly love the Lord. My intention with *The Rib Connection* is to unplug the censored silence that has been placed on these subjects and provide what I hope is a platform for real deliverance for all people who struggle in the area of relationships.

A lot of money is being spent on religious performance and entertainment that leave one hyped but not helped, perspired but not inspired. God loves His people and He wants to help them at a dimension far beyond what they have experienced and expected so far. *The Rib Connection* is not the only answer, but it is a revelation resource that I pray God will use to put the world on the road to restoration and recovery. Join me in this effort to blow the devil out of the family of God and place him where he belongs, under the feet of healthy and happy relationships.

Carlos L. Malone, Sr.
May, 2007

Introduction

PRACTICAL PRINCIPLES FROM ADAM'S RIB

Birthed out of the passionate womb of need and desire comes the dread of desperation. In our quest to avoid the longevity of loneliness, we are tempted to take matters into our own hands when it comes to marital mating. For whatever reason, whether it be the tradition of their upbringing, or the temptation of a restless and uncontrollable flesh, many people rush quickly into marriage.

Those within the church who do so often grab strongly onto the apostle Paul's biblical exhortation to the immature believers in Corinth: "But I say unto the unmarried and to the widows: It is good for them if they remain even as I am; but if they cannot exercise self-control, let them marry. For it is better to marry than to burn with passion" (1 Cor. 7:8-9). Contrary to what many may assume, however, this passage in no way suggests that one should enter into a covenant relationship of marriage based solely upon the freedom to exercise uncontrollable sexual urges. To do so would be both immature and unadvised.

Paul's emphasis here is, indeed, the very opposite. He is not talking about sexual freedom, but about self-control. Marriage is more than just sex (as you will discover in this book). It is a lifetime of covenant, compassion, commitment, and consecration, all of which require that we be mature enough and Spirit-filled enough to seek the God who created us, to get His input and involvement in our selection of a mate for marriage. God alone knows His perfect will is for us. We must without hesitation seek God the Father for His guidance and governance concerning our marital status. We have to let God do it.

Marriage was not Adam's good idea, but God's divine answer to a compassionate desire that He had for Adam (man). Before Eve came along, Adam had no idea of his aloneness or his need for a mate. How could he? He could not miss what he had never had. Adam did not struggle with sexual fantasies or erotic dreams; he had no point of reference for doing so. God Himself, who created man for His glory, determined that it was not good for the man to be alone.

Notice that the word is "alone," not "lonely"; you can be alone and yet never be lonely. Adam was not empty or unfulfilled being alone, but God decided to enhance the quality of Adam's life by giving him someone for his own glory. What Adam was to God, woman would be to Adam. God caused a deep sleep to overshadow Adam, and through a sovereign surgical procedure, God created for man a woman who became his helper and wife. This is what I call, "Adam's Rib."

So take this journey with me and study some practical principles that will help you gain a deeper understanding of relationships and marriage. I pray that through the Holy Spirit's power, and your openness as a reader, fresh revelation and insight will release into your spirit a deeper understanding and appreciation for the covenant of marriage, whether you currently are married or single. If you are single and seeking, I pray also that this book will help you find wisdom and discernment so that when the time is right, you can make the right "Rib Connection."

CHAPTER ONE

Let God Do It

One of the most valuable lessons that we can ever learn in life is the lesson of praying about everything. We were created to depend on God. It was never the intent of the Almighty to have us function in the world without a relationship with Him. The medium that makes that relationship is communication. It is through prayer that we develop a personal relationship with God that will cause us to come to know His voice and His ways. I do not take lightly the importance of knowing the Word of God, but I would like to suggest also that there is a distinct difference between knowing the Word of God and knowing the God of the Word.

Prayer affords us the opportunity of getting to know God personally. Many significant things happen when we have a praying relationship with God, but the two that I believe are of the greatest importance are faith and trust. My faith in God is my belief in him as God. My trust in God speaks to my confidence in Him. It is through my faith that hope harbors in my heart, and through trust that I experience peace. When we have a relationship with God that is based on faith and trust, we develop a true sense of dependency that will cause us to include Him in every decision we make in life.

Here is where so many of us get off course. When it comes to dating and mating, we have the tendency to exclude God from the picture until we have made our selection, and then we seek God's approval. Let's be honest: many relationships end in disaster because of a poor choice. Traditional marriage vows end with the declaration: "Whom God hath joined together, let no man put asunder." This declaration speaks directly to the power of divine joining or connection. When God puts something together, it's supposed to remain together. When a man and a woman join themselves to each other in holy matrimony, they are supposed to stay joined. God made marriage, and only He can unmake it.

God made marriage, and only He can unmake it.

This does not mean that married couples never struggle or have disagreements. What it does mean is that in marriage we must find our strength and support for survival in the power of the God who joined us to each other. For this reason, it is so important when choosing a mate that we consult God *before* the search begins. When it comes to finding a spouse, most people take matters into their own hands. For that matter, we tend to handle all our relationships that way, following human and fleshly attraction rather than godly and spiritual instruction. This is one cause for many failed marriages. It certainly is not the only reason, but let's face it: it's hard to stay with a person God never intended us to be with.

I am certain that many marriage clinicians would disagree with me on this, but I am convinced that if we expect God to bless it, we need to include Him in the initial selection. Proverbs 3: 5-6 says, "Trust in the Lord with all your heart, And lean not on your own understanding; In all your ways acknowledge Him, and He shall direct your paths." This is not a post-application, but a pre-application Scripture. Don't wait until you have entered into covenantal agreement before you seek God. Seek Him first, because He already knows what and whom He has purposed for your life. God is never confused or indecisive; He is always accurate and assured.

FATHER KNOWS BEST

In Genesis chapter two, God initiates the process of mating for Adam in the garden. It begins with God's observation that, "It is not good that man be alone; I will make him a help comparable to him" (Gen. 2:18). Notice that it is God who will make a mate for the man; Adam was not going to go out, hunt one up, and bring her to God for His blessing. God took the job upon Himself.

In the same way, it is important that every person who seeks or hopes for marriage seeks God first. The first step to dating and mating is constant prayer and spiritual counseling. Do not follow the foolish wisdom of the world that would suggest that you keep dating until you find the right person. Do you have any idea how much time,

Relationships built wholly or mostly around sex rarely last.

emotions, and "yes money" you could waste trying to figure out who the "right" person is? So many times we commit our emotions to someone before we take the time to evaluate that person and seek the wisdom of God.

And God forbid that you make the mistake of becoming sexually involved with the person before marriage; that makes it almost impossible to hear God. This is due to the fact that sex is a very powerful part of human emotion and desire, so powerful, in fact, that God designed it to be limited to the consummation of marriage. When you become sexually involved with someone before marriage, you could easily end up choosing your mate based upon his or her sexual performance, particularly if the sex was fulfilling and gratifying. Relationships built wholly or mostly around sex rarely last. Seasoned married couples will tell you that although sex is very important in a marriage, it will never keep a marriage together. Being connected to the person that God created for you is the essence of what will cause you to stay together.

I can still remember February 1978 vividly. I had been dating Pamela since July 1977, the same year I had begun my preaching ministry. As a young man struggling to overcome a past filled with a lot of sexual promiscuity, I realized that the call of God on my life for ministry meant that I needed to make some drastic changes in my life. No matter how much I liked Pamela, I knew I needed to seek God for guidance in this matter. At twenty, my hormones were off the hook. I did not want to lead Pamela on, nor did I want to consume my life with a relationship that had no future.

It was a cold and snowy Sunday, with an ice storm predicted. I decided to visit the church where I had grown up and been baptized because it was closer to my aunt's house, where I was staying at the time. So that Pamela would not look for me in vain, I had informed her that I would not be at our regular church that Sunday.

Upon arriving at the church, I was taken to the pastor, a man with whom I had a great relationship. To my surprise, he had come down with the flu and did not feel up to preaching. He also had no assistant that he felt he could call on to preach without prior notice. So he asked me if I would preach for him that morning. I couldn't say no, regardless of how afraid I felt. I had only been preaching nine months, so fear was something I was dealing with still.

The pastor left me in his office so that I could pray and prepare. As I prepared to pray, the thought occurred to me that this would be the first sermon I had ever preached where Pamela was not there. A little while later, as I sat on the platform near the pulpit, I prayed to the Lord very sincerely, "If Pamela is the girl that I am to spend the rest of my life with, let her come to this church service." Within five minutes, she walked through the door. Needless to say, I was hoping she would, but had she not come through that door, I was prepared to let her go.

Pamela and I have been married now for twenty-seven years, and, due to the challenges and the changes that all marriages go through, there have been many times when we have wondered whether we missed God in our decision. No, marriage has not always been easy, but through all the hurt and pain we have caused each other, we have been able to survive the test and stay together because we have recognized that, even as different as we are, we have been joined together by the purpose of God. We have learned that no matter how challenging the times might become, we can survive any storm when God is on board and standing as the joint that keeps us together.

ARE YOU "CUT OUT" FOR MARRIAGE?

One of the other noticeable things about the Genesis 2 account is that the woman that God gave to Adam was a woman that was made from his rib. She came out of his side and was fashioned for him. Before choosing a mate, it is important for you to know if God has purposed you to be married. Not every man is cut out for a wife, and not every woman is cut out for a husband. If you are considering this step, let me urge you to check yourself thoroughly and be honest with yourself concerning this matter of marriage.

> *Before choosing a mate, it is important for you to know if God has purposed you to be married.*

Men, we must be certain that we *have* a missing rib. Likewise, ladies, you must be certain that you *are* a missing rib. A successful marriage calls for a lot of unselfish sacrifice on both sides, as you will see as you begin on this journey. Some men are too egotistical, self-centered and irresponsible to make good husbands, while some women are too spoiled, insensitive and insecure to become good wives.

Don't automatically assume marriage is for you. Check with God first and find out from Him what His will is concerning you. Perhaps you are a person whom God has chosen to be single and saved just for Himself. If this is the case, you must find a way to have peace with the knowledge that the most important thing in your life is not to be married, but to be purposeful for God. Someone might ask, "But how do I deal with and control all those natural, God-given, hormone-driven desires?" If God has chosen you for Himself only, He will provide you with the strength and power to overcome all of the fleshly desires and longings that you will have. But take heart: the reward is greater for those who have been given this challenge, because they have to overcome so much more than the person who has a spouse.

When you allow Almighty God to sovereignly select your mate, He then has a vested interest to cause great and mighty things to happen between you. Little do many couples know that marriage is more of a spiritual connection than it is physical. I strongly encourage all young persons who desire to be married to wait for a while before you start searching. Take your time. Spend some quality time seeking God's guidance. We spend a lot of time choosing the right college. We devote years of preparation, study and research to earn our degree. We expend great amounts of time, energy and effort searching for the right job and career. We take extreme care finding the right house to buy, and even get a real estate agent to assist us. If we are so careful in all these things, why should we be less attentive and responsible when it comes to choosing a mate?

Allow God and the counsel of your pastor or some other qualified person help you in this matter. Marriage is serious business and should be taken seriously. The choice you make will be the choice that you will have to live with. Don't look at marriage as something that you can get out of if it doesn't work. Learn to view marriage the same way God does: a lifelong covenant between two persons (male/female) and their God, destined to bring glory to each other. Your chance of survival in marriage is 100% if you let God create it, cover it, and control it. *Just let God do it.* It will survive. I am a living witness to that truth.

CHAPTER TWO

If It Don't Fit, Don't Pray For It

————◆◆◆————

O ne of the most pride-pricking, ego-embarrassing and discouraging things in life is the realization that you have made a bad choice. It is hard to give up on something or someone when you are "sure" that you had God's go-ahead sign. Allow me to clear the air of a spiritual misunderstanding: *missing God is not a sign of spiritual immaturity; it is a sign of growth.* If there is one thing I have discovered after twenty-nine years in ministry, with twenty-four of those years as a senior pastor, it is that were it not for my mistakes, I would have very little to preach about. Except for my mistakes, I would never have learned how to hear God or to recognize when He is speaking to me.

So many times in our lives we get ahead of God. Anxious desires have been the cause of many persons making hasty decisions without careful evaluation. Some people (especially women) are so intent on getting married that they allow the hurry and hustle of their hormones to cause them to make decisions they find impossible to live with later. And all the while, truth was speaking to them while they were dating, but because they were investing so much of themselves into the relationship, they did not watch for, or simply ignored, the signs that told them the truth.

Truth is something that not many people want to hear when they are traveling down the road of a wrong decision. The danger with many people when it comes to relationships is that they try to make a right turn from the left lane. Trying to make something happen that is not meant to be is a very dangerous thing. Where marriage is concerned, it can never be, "I think so," or. "I am not sure." It *has* to be, "Yes, I am ready," or, "No, I will wait." Marriage is too important for you to allow anyone or anything to pressure you into it before you are ready. Why are you praying about marrying someone who does not share your values, virtues and vision?

Marriage is too important for you to allow anyone or anything to pressure you into it before you are ready.

You would be foolish to buy a car simply because it looks good sitting on the dealer's lot. If you're smart, you will check the miles, get the maintenance history of the vehicle, and see how many owners it has had. A fancy paint job may be impressive, but that's inexpensive labor. More important is to make sure the car runs well and can get you where you are going when you need to get there. After all, you buy a car for the long term, not the short term. Remember, "If It Don't Fit, Don't Pray For It."

USE CARE WHEN CHOOSING YOUR MATE

Choosing a mate is a very serious, life-changing decision, much more serious than buying a car. The person with whom you are considering spending the rest of your life must be someone you not only love, but also like. It is important that the two of you share some major commonality. Neither of you have to like everything the other one likes, but you should share a common liking for the major things. For example, when it comes to things like family, money, religion, sex, children, etc., your views must concur, not conflict. Unless you take these matters seriously when choosing a mate, you will set yourself up for many years of hardship and regret.

God created marriage as a beautiful and intimate relationship between a man and a woman who share the same goals and values. Marriage never comes without baggage, but both partners should be fully aware of each other's baggage before the marriage begins. Many of the things that married couples typically fight over are issues that could have and should have been dealt with before the wedding. So many times, men and women both allow physical attraction to blind them, causing them not to see the person they are marrying for who that person truly is. When choosing your mate, don't overlook anything, because anything you overlook now, you will have to continue to overlook after you are married.

I'm not suggesting that you can find the "perfect" person—no one meets that standard—but I am suggesting that you can find the perfect *match*. No one buys two left shoes or two right gloves, or one left slip-on shoe and one right lace-up shoe. No, everything must match perfectly before you choose it. So how do we find the perfect match in a mate? To answer that question, let's look at the manner by which God chose a mate for Adam and see how these "ribs" can connect us to some truths and principles that can help us make better choices in our relationships.

COMPLETION OR COMPLEMENTARY?

Genesis 2:18 (KJV) reads: "And the Lord God said, It is not good that the man should be alone; I will make him an help meet for him." One thing that is clear about the creation narratives in the Book of Genesis is that Yahweh declared that everything He had created was good. This verse, however, reveals that God had observed the man's aloneness and determined that it was *not* good. Up to this point everything had been good. Now Yahweh must fix the problem of Adam's aloneness.

In order to understand this in clearer detail, we must study this text in the original Hebrew. For instance, in Hebrew, the words for "help meet" mean a "helper corresponding to him," or, a "corresponding helper" for the man. This word "helper" is not a demeaning term; the Bible uses it frequently of God Himself, who "helps" mankind. The description of woman as corresponding to man means, basically, that what was said about him in Genesis 2:7 was also true of her: "And the LORD God formed man of the dust of the ground, and breathed into his nostrils the breath of life; and man became a living being." In other words, they both had the same nature. But what the man lacked, she supplied, and what she lacked, he supplied.

The two of you must complement each other.

If a man is going to have a wife and a woman is going to have a husband, they ought to possess the ability to help each other as a couple. No one needs to be married to someone who does not in any way complement or help him or her. God is not the author of confusion, so be advised that He will never link you to someone you cannot get along or go along with. The two of you must complement each other.

I know there are Bible readers who would disagree with that statement in light of the story of Hosea and Gomer in the Book of Hosea. However, Hosea's and Gomer's experience is not God's norm for marriage, and besides, the Book of Hosea is more about God proving his love for Israel despite her adulterous ways towards Him. God used the marriage of the prophet Hosea to Gomer as an illustration of how He was being treated by the people whom He had chosen to love. The Book of Hosea does not provide a standard for marriage.

The apostle Paul, on the other hand, specifically instructs believers not to be "unequally yoked" with non-believers: "Do not be unequally yoked together with unbelievers. For what fellowship has righteousness with lawlessness? And what communion has light with darkness? And what accord has Christ with Belial? Or what part has a believer with an unbeliever?" (2 Cor. 6:14-15). In the things that really matter, it is impossible for a believer and an unbeliever to complement each other. True marriage in all its fullness as God intended cannot be obtained in such a relationship.

Some may be confused about the difference between completing and complementing. It is my firm conviction that no one should marry with the intention of finding someone who will "complete" them. When two persons of the opposite sex come together in marriage, each of them should already be a "complete" person. In other words, you are not ready for marriage until you know who you are and why you are here, and until you are completely fulfilled within yourself and your relationship with God.

If you marry someone who is unfulfilled and incomplete in his or her personal identity, you will always be burdened with having to deal with that person's insecurities. In that kind of situation, how do you know who you are marrying? When you take this risk, you also run the risk of that person changing into someone you do not like. I could not begin to count the number of times I have heard someone say, "If only I had known that he (or she) was like that, I would have never married him (or her)." By then it's too late. You have a marriage covenant to uphold, children to raise, and mutual responsibilities to fulfill, and the fact that the two of you are like oil and water makes it even harder. The whole thing could have been avoided had you applied in the beginning the principles of wisdom and patience.

Why would you spend time praying to God for what He has not purposed for you? Always remember that your desire for your life must be His design for your life. Jesus said, "If you abide in Me, and My words abide in you, you will ask what you desire, and it shall be done for you" (Jn. 15:7). Many people misrepresent this verse as giving them permission to pray for anything under the sun that they desire. The proper interpretation of Jesus' words is that we can get whatever we ask for as long as our request is in alignment with God's Word, which is also His will. God does not have a will for you beyond His Word, so make sure that your wishes are in line with His

Word. This is why Jesus said, *"If you abide in Me..."* because if you abide in Him, you will always know what His perfect will is for you.

COME INTO AGREEMENT WITH YOUR PARTNER BEFORE THE WEDDING

The purpose of a mate in marriage is to complement, not complete you. Don't marry with the expectation of affirmation. When two people marry, they each come into the relationship with different ideas and dreams. What the two of them must do (with the husband leading the way) is sit together and prayerfully seek the guidance of Almighty God. This is why both of you should be born-again, Spirit-filled believers in Christ.

Ideally, this prayerful discussion of visions and dreams should take place long before the marriage begins. If the two of you discover that you can't come to a cooperative conclusion on the direction that your relationship should go, it would be best for you to wait until you *can* agree; otherwise, consider walking away from the relationship. The Bible says that two cannot walk together except they agree (Amos 3:3). It makes no sense (or cents) to have an expensive wedding and a cheap marriage that doesn't last because the two people involved can't seem to agree on the things that are most important for building and maintaining a healthy relationship.

Many people make the tragic mistake of believing that if they pray, God will make them come into agreement. That is partially true; God can make anything happen. But He will not *make* us agree with each other; that is a point of our free will. God does not go around making us agree with Him. Instead, He gives us the freedom to choose, along with the consequences that come with our choice.

The power of choice can be extremely fruitful, but it can also be fatal. That is why it is so important that we take advantage of the freedom that God gives us, and exercise great care and wisdom in our decisions. Don't wait until you have already made a commitment to someone to begin asking questions. The time for questions is long before the wedding takes place. Afterwards is almost always too late.

ALWAYS BE YOURSELF

Choosing a mate does not in any way mean losing your own identity. Who you are is far more important than who you marry. One thing is sure: you can never escape the truth of who you are, not even in marriage. This is why you need to *know* who you are before you get married. Otherwise, you and your spouse will be in for a big (and perhaps ugly) surprise when the true you comes out at some point.

Don't change who you are just to fit into some type of unfamiliar or uncomfortable role. Self-acceptance and self-appreciation both are valuable lessons in life. Whenever you make a decision to change, make sure that it is because you feel the need to change and not because someone wants to change you. So many people make the tragic mistake of entering into a relationship with a person they feel they can change. *It won't happen!* Psychologists tell us that our personalities and identities are firmly established by the time we are twelve, if not earlier. Any of us can change what we do, but it is a major undertaking to change who we are.

The time for questions is long before the wedding takes place.

Learn to be comfortable being yourself. Who you are is what makes you different from everyone else. One of the ways to tell that the person you are considering is right for you is if that person does not have to change anything about himself or herself in order to be with you—and when you feel no pressure to change for the sake of that other person. Don't make the mistake of believing that you can choose someone and expect God to change him or her for you. If you hope to live peaceably with someone, you must allow that someone to be the person he or she is becoming by the grace of God.

Most of us are being changed by virtue of God's plan for our lives. He knows what it will take for us to become what He has purposed. The priority of our lives is God's purpose for our lives. Stop trying to mold people into what you would have them to be. Extend your search and be patient. God will send to you the person that is perfect for you; a person who will change anything about himself or herself in order to be with you.

The thing that has caused me to love my wife Pamela, and to be so much at peace around her, is the fact that I stopped trying to change her into something that I wanted her to be. I've had to learn to love her for who she is. (And she had to do the same with me.) This takes so much pressure off the relationship and off each of us. My whole prayer focus concerning my wife and my life has changed. I have learned to trust God, who knows what I need and fashions everything about my life around His divine purpose for me.

Adam never approached God about a woman; God gave him what he needed. Learn to trust God with your whole life. Don't let your flesh cause you to make a foolish decision that will leave you with a frustrated life. Know that God is in your corner, willing only good things for you. Allow His Spirit and power to guide you in everything. And remember: *If it doesn't fit, don't pray for it!*

A PRAYER

Dear heavenly Father, I thank You for being a true Father. You are always there to guide and direct us. I thank You that as Your children we have access to You by faith. Father, I ask you to invoke Your people with Your powerful hand of influence. So often we do not realize that You are there for us even when we have to make decisions concerning relationship matters. I ask that through Your Spirit we will find our way to You. May we come to know that You know what is best for us and You want what is best for us. Relieve us of the pressure of having to make choices by ourselves, and lead us to see You as a loving Father, ready to help and to guide. All praise and glory be unto you, Father, in the name of Jesus. Amen.

CHAPTER THREE

The Love Connection

———⟩•⟨———

We hear it over and over again. It is perhaps the most oft-spoken phrase in the world, voiced by millions every day. What is this phrase? It is the statement, "I love you." We say these words so easily, yet I often wonder if we really know what love is, and if we do, how often we demonstrate it in its truest sense.

For many people, love is simply an emotion filled with passion and sensuality. While that certainly describes one facet of love, there is far more to love than just an emotional feeling. Love goes much deeper than emotions. Because so many people are so confused and so ill-informed as to the true nature of love, we will consider in this chapter several primary aspects of this subject. Some may prove to be both controversial and argumentative, while others will be straight to the point. In this chapter I hope to challenge you to consider love from a more detailed and in-depth sense, especially in the way you express it to another person.

True love is what guarantees and authenticates all human relationships. Any relationship that loses love loses the ability to survive. Where true love abounds, however, survival is virtually guaranteed. If you are seeking the secret to a strong, healthy, and lasting relationship, I challenge you to pay close attention to this chapter so that you may be assured of making the right "love connection."

WHAT IS THE LOVE CONNECTION?

When we speak of being connected to something or someone, we usually have in mind being joined or attached together, either physically or figuratively. In the context of this book, we can understand love as the power that makes and sustains the connection between two persons who are seeking a relationship with each other.

No true love connection can exist unless both persons are spiritually connected.

There are several ways and many different words we can use to define love. For example, the Greeks have at least four different words for love, the greatest of which is *agapao*, which refers specifically to the God-kind of love. With reference to God, *agapao* expresses the deep and constant love and interest of a perfect being towards entirely unworthy objects, producing and fostering a reciprocal and reverential love in them towards the giver. As it relates to believers, *agapao*, or, Christian love, whether exercised toward the brethren or toward men generally, is not an impulse from the feelings. *Agapao* does not always run with the natural inclinations. In fact, it almost never does. This kind of love seeks the welfare of all men, especially those who are of the household of faith. It is not prejudiced, but crosses all racial and religious boundaries, extending itself to all who will receive it.

The love connection between two persons of the opposite sex is a trichotomy in its form, touching spirit, mind, and body. No true love connection can exist unless both persons are spiritually connected. Two persons who are headed in different directions spiritually are on a collision course with conflict and disaster. In biblical marriage, as God designed it, a man and a woman unite spiritually, committing themselves to each other under the sanction and blessings of Almighty God.

It is essential that these two persons be connected with regard to their spiritual beliefs, because the key to any successful relationship is its spiritual foundation. Whenever a conflict occurs between each person's fundamental and practical spiritual principles, the foundation of the relationship is shaken and may become weakened to the point of being unable to survive. This is an area that is often very problematic, because of our misguided human tendency to neglect or underestimate the importance of spiritual commonality in a relationship. Whatever their religious beliefs, any couple contemplating marriage must have the same spiritual connection so that they can avoid spiritual conflict.

As a Christian man married to a Christian woman, I can say without hesitation that had it not been for my spiritual beliefs and the spiritual connection between my wife and me, we would not have survived twenty-five years of marriage. The survival of our marriage has required a lot of forgiveness, patience, longsuffering, understanding and support. Our ability to embrace these virtues comes from the well of our spiritual foundation.

Only God can empower you to forgive and forget when another person has wronged you. It takes the power of the Holy Spirit to be intimate with someone who has recently said some very harsh and hurtful things to you. But when there is a connection of the Spirit between the two of you, God will get you back on track and keep you there.

One way He does this is through conviction. He shows you your shortcomings and how often He has had to pardon you of your sins. He shows you the many times He had to cover your mess and clean it up. He reminds you when you get impatient with your spouse how He has endured your inconsistencies and supported you through all of the transitions that it has taken you to get to that place of maturity. I cannot express strongly enough the importance of making and maintaining your spiritual love connection with the person with whom you are in a relationship.

THE SPIRITUAL CONNECTION IS VITAL!

Fulfilling the roles and responsibilities that come with being married will require the help of the Holy Spirit. For instance, there is the very real challenge of remaining faithful to your mate and resisting the temptation to stray into the arms of another lover. Every marriage relationship, no matter how much love is present, comes under this kind of fire and testing. It seems as though men generally find this more of a problem to face than women do, although women certainly are not immune. It takes more than love to keep from falling into this trap; staying faithful requires the power and discipline of the Holy Spirit.

Submission is another example. The Bible plainly states that a woman is to submit to her husband. "Submit" is a very strong word, particularly the way most people understand it today. Godly submission of a woman to her husband is not possible in the flesh. Only the power of the Holy Spirit can help a woman who has independent abilities and gifts submit to her husband. Within her human nature is the tendency to act differently, but her spiritual nature in Christ helps her to find it easy to comply. This is especially true when her husband submits himself to her in a self-sacrificial way, just as Jesus did for His bride, the church.

When a husband and wife are connected this way spiritually, their desire is not just to please themselves or each other, but also to please the God whom they serve. Being connected in the Spirit carries privileges, promises and power. Do not allow your longing for a love connection cause you to neglect the importance of the spiritual connection. The two go together. This is an important point to remember, because when God created man, He did not make him a body with a spirit, but a spirit with a body.

The remarkable thing about Adam and Eve is how they could be in love, since, prior to being joined as one, they had not spent any time together. They had never been on a date and had not had time to learn each other's habits, good or bad. So what was their connection? Let's review the facts from the Genesis narrative:

And the Lord God caused a deep sleep to fall on Adam, and he slept; and He took one of his ribs, and closed up the flesh in its place. Then the rib which the Lord God had taken from man He made into a woman, and He brought her to the man. And Adam said: "This is now bone of my bones And flesh of my flesh; She shall be called Woman, Because she was taken out of Man." Therefore a man shall leave his father and mother and be joined to his wife, and they shall become one flesh. And they were both naked, the man and his wife, and were not ashamed (Genesis 2:21-25).

Adam understood God and knew that whatever God had given him was the perfect gift. His knowledge of God's love for him, and his love for God, made it easy for him to embrace this new species that he called "woman." The fact that God created her for him *from* him made the connection even easier and more acceptable. I'd like to suggest that their connection was their acceptance of and obedience to the will of God for their lives. When we are truly spiritual, our primary aim always is to please God *first*. The spiritual nature that God gave Adam and Eve is what enabled each of them to walk in their roles as husband and wife without debate or shame over their nakedness.

> *In God's eyes, love is both sacred and sacrificial.*

LOVE: SACRED AND SACRIFICIAL

Let's talk a little more about love. In God's eyes, love is both sacred and sacrificial. These are the qualities of the love He shows toward us. Love is sacred in what it represents and sacrificial in how it relates to others. The sacredness of love is seen in the fact that it is the essence of God's nature and being. First John 4:8 says that God is love; so then, love is not just what God does, but who God is.

One of the most profound and beautiful things about love is that it finds its fulfillment not in what it receives but in what it gives. When you love someone, you are more interested in what you can do for the one you love than in what that person can do for you. When you are connected to a person by love, you find more joy in being able to bring fulfillment to that person than in being fulfilled yourself. This is the sacrificial aspect of love, when you unselfishly put the interest of others ahead of your own.

Love looks more on the needs of others than on its own needs. The unselfishness of love is clearly seen in how God loved us even before we were able to love Him back. As a matter of personal knowledge, He loved me *until* I could love him back. When I had no desire for Him, He was yet pursuing me with love, giving me chance after chance. This is the kind of love that God wants us to have one for another, whether in simple friendship or in the realm of marriage.

Many relationships and marriages have been destroyed because of the unwillingness of one or both persons to sacrifice for the good of the other. Marriage carries with it the obligation for both partners to make the necessary sacrifices to please their mates. According to 1 Corinthians 13:5, love is not self-seeking in nature, but strives and aims to please others. This is a reference to *Agape*, or the God-kind of love, but it is also a principle that should be displayed in every area of our lives.

It should be the desire of every husband and wife to give subserviently to each other. When they both understand the power of servanthood, submission to each other and support of each other's needs and desires become easy. I am of the firm belief that whatever my wife's desires and needs are, be they financial, sexual, emotional, spiritual or physical, it should be my desire and duty to do all that I can to fulfill those needs.

The question then becomes, where is the limit? Where do we draw the line? When it comes to needs, in marriage there *are* no limits! I've heard many persons say that they find it hard to do certain things in their relationships because of their beliefs. This is another reason why it is so important that you dialogue about your beliefs and values before you marry so you will know what to expect. Patience is definitely a virtue, particularly during the transition from single life to married life, but make sure you transition by communicating with each other and involving each other in the process. Support each other with loving care and tender words while you are making adjustments that are not comfortable.

When it comes to needs, in marriage there are no limits!

Discomfort of this nature is most common in the sexual dimension of the relationship. Most couples agree on and desire more money, more communication, and more material things; we all want these things and it doesn't make anyone uncomfortable when talking about them (except, perhaps, about when and where to spend money). Sex, on the other hand, is something that many men and women are in bondage about, when it is the very thing that consummates the marriage. We will discuss this in greater detail later on in the chapters dealing with his needs vs. her needs.

Love knows no boundaries and is ready and willing at all times to serve and support the needs of others. We must have that spiritual connection with the Father in order to make the love connection. Jesus said that when we are in a relationship with Him, we have the power to love, honor and obey (see Jn. 15: 9-17). When we are truly connected to love, we possess unlimited power within us to overcome anything and everything that comes our way in life. Love has ruling and controlling power that inspires us to do things we said we would never do. Paul said in 2 Corinthians 5:14, that the love of God constrains us. This means exactly what it says: to control, to impel, to urge. God's love for us is the love that we are supposed to have for each other.

There is no way around it: the love connection is what makes the difference in a relationship and determines the life of the relationship. Be sure to connect to a person before you commit to that person. Otherwise, you could end up connected to someone who is not connected to you. The principle is the same whether you are married or single, and whether the relationship is with a spouse, a friend, a co-worker, a relative, a prospective mate, or whoever. Check your knowledge of love and be sure that you understand the basic principles, and then apply them to your life, judging and scoring yourself fairly during the process. For those of you who are seeking to be married, make sure that you embrace the truths in this chapter as a source of wisdom to guide you as you make the Love Connection in your life.

A PRAYER

Heavenly Father, thank You for being the only true example of what it means to love. You have loved us with so much longsuffering and forbearance that we're amazed even the more. Father, teach us daily the importance and power of unconditional love, breaking those religious barriers that we have concerning each other. Help us to know that the world is filled with all kinds of people and all kinds of issues, but yet You gave Your son to die for it. Forgive us of the sins that cause us to be hypocritical toward each other, and teach us not to be discriminatory, racist, hateful, or judgmental of each other. Thank you for never giving up on us, but loving us through the rough times of our process. Open our eyes, that we may see the scars within ourselves and seek You for healing of our emotions and will. Bless our existing marriages and those soon to be born. Grant those of us who are still single the wisdom to choose accurately and wisely. Bless You, Father, and all praise is given unto you, In Jesus' Name, Amen.

CHAPTER FOUR

The Danger of Compromise

———⊳•⊲———

Compromise is a strong word with lasting effects and, in some cases, eternal consequences. A compromise is when two parties come to a mutual agreement where both parties have sacrificed something. Compromise of this type involves concessions on both sides. In the worlds of politics, business, and other arenas of human interaction, compromise is often necessary and may even be healthy. Compromise on the personal level, however, is another story. Sacrificing one's principles, values, and standards on the altars of convenience and expediency can be disastrous—and even deadly. That is the kind of compromise we will be discussing in this chapter.

Whenever you compromise your beliefs, you make yourself a vulnerable target for those who do not have your best interest at heart. There are times when compromise is good and necessary for the sake of preserving a meaningful relationship. Compromise is completely acceptable in areas of life where flexibility exists, such as philosophies, wants and desires, because these things may be influenced by one's environment. Some things we because of the environment we are exposed to, while other behaviors are due to the evolution of our personality, which determines who we are and what we are becoming.

Every person is born into this world with his or her own distinct personality. Your personality is what defines you as a person. One reason many relationships and marriages hit the rocks with no room to recover is because one partner or the other, or both, spent too much time trying to change the other one into someone he or she was not. This is always a lost cause, and death to a relationship. Never compromise who you are as a person for the sake of a relationship, particularly with someone who wants to change you but is not willing to allow you the same privilege.

Never compromise who you are as a person for the sake of a relationship.

When someone asks me, "How do I know if this person is right for me?" one of the things I always say is: "When that person does not have to change who he or she is in order to be with you." Accepting people for who they are is one of the most important keys to a healthy relationship. It takes a mature mind to understand that you don't enter into a relationship with a person who has one personality, and then demand him or her to change down the road. So many times we commit to the "outer courts" of a person, and never go into the "inner courts" of his or her personality, those deep places where the guilt and regrets of an imperfect life are carefully shielded from view.

Looking only at a person, rather than into a person, limits the information you have to work with in making a wise decision. Don't make the mistake that many people make: they limit their questions about each other while dating, and wait until after they are married to maximize their research. It is only after they have purchased the product, taken it home, unwrapped it, and played with it for a few years, that they discover to their dismay that they are not satisfied. Then they want to return it for a full refund. Unfortunately, it doesn't work like that. They have compromised a valuable principle that says, "Read the label before you purchase this product, to be sure that you are not allergic to it."

People are not like household appliances; we can't use them for a while until they no longer satisfy and then trade them in for a replacement. Human relationships call for much greater sensitivity than that. So how do we avoid this kind of situation? By exercising caution and discernment from the beginning, and by a firm commitment not to compromise our principles, standards, and values. With this in mind, let's take a closer look at the world of compromise and why it is so dangerous.

UNDERSTANDING VALUE

One of the "wisdom quotes" I often use when counseling people with low self-esteem issues, is: *"If you do not have an understanding of your self worth, you'll either sell yourself cheap or give yourself away free."* Compromise becomes a genuine danger when the "real you" is not taken seriously by the person with whom you are in a relationship; when that person fails to appreciate or respect you as a person of value in your own right. So many times, desperate people discount who they are—cheapen themselves—just so that they can fit in with someone who has nothing to offer by way of a meaningful relationship. When you do not know the value of your stock, you take away all the future possibilities of living a life of complete happiness and total fulfillment as an individual.

> *If no one "purchases a ticket" to see you, buy one for yourself, and feel good about yourself.*

Notice that I said, "individual," which implies that you have to know yourself, believe in yourself, and appreciate yourself for who you are, even if no one else does. If no one "purchases a ticket" to see you, buy one for yourself, and feel good about yourself. In time, you will watch yourself become a person of substance.

Before you can even begin to think seriously about committing to any relationship, let alone marriage, you've got to get yourself together. Stop believing that you must have someone else to affirm you, authenticate you, or tell you that it's all right to be yourself. People who need this kind of external support are emotionally and psychologically unhealthy, and destined for many failed relationships.

What brings balance to a good relationship is when two persons who are involved with each other have a confident understanding of who they are as individuals and what they want out of life. This eliminates a lot of stress in the relationship because neither partner will have to carry pacifiers or Pampers to give out when the other acts like a spoiled child, whining, crying, and throwing a tantrum because of not getting his or her own way. If you do not understand your own value, you can become a very "heavy" person.

"Heavy" people are needy people who weigh you down with their constant need to be affirmed and motivated, and when you do not cater to their needs, the first thing they say is, "You don't care." The real problem is not that you don't care about them, but that you just don't care to carry them all the time, when they were created to carry themselves. That's why God gave us legs as part of our human anatomy, as well as a brain with awesome intellectual potential, so that we could carry our own weight. Carriers are for infants and the immature, so stop depending on others to validate your value. Know your own worth and secure it without compromise.

At the same time, be careful of your exposure. When people see something of value, they try to find a cheap way to purchase it. You have to know that you are expensive and that not everybody can afford you. This is not to say that you are above people, just that you are above people who try to put you beneath them by attempting to make you feel cheap. When God sought to purchase you, He paid a great price: the very life of His Son. You are an expensive, even priceless, piece of goods; don't sell yourself at a flea market or dollar store price. Know your worth and protect yourself at all cost, even if it means eliminating those relationships that are not promoting your good. Drop those persons as fast as the prices drop at a blue-light special at K-Mart.

To all my sisters out there, let me say this: when God made you, He put a man to sleep, cut him deep, took out one of his ribs, and made you. When the man awakened out of his deep sleep, he called you woman, because you were cut out of him, leaving a womb. Then you became what is called, "female." You are not called a "free male," because you come with a fee, and a costly fee, if you know your value.

Let me say to all my brothers that when God created you, He created a man of substance, power and creative ability. Don't allow the desires of your flesh to cause you to lower your standards or compromise who you are. When you know your value, you compromise neither your standards nor your convictions. Know your value, stand on your convictions, and make it impossible for anyone to take the advantage of you.

GETTING TO KNOW YOU

Getting to know yourself is the first step toward developing a greater sense of value toward yourself. Self-knowledge increases your personal awareness and appreciation of who you are as an individual. Individuality is a gift that God the Creator has given to each of us. There is no one else like you, so the only person you will ever be in competition with is yourself.

Knock, Knock. Who's there? It's you, trapped behind the walls of uncertainty and insecurity, blinded by an overrated appraisal of others while defeated by an underrated appraisal of yourself. Learn to listen to the "true you" inside you, your true inner self with its ingenious intellect, yearning to be released to fulfill itself instead of wasting away inside your body. Why feed on need constantly instead of making it your business to get to know yourself and accept yourself for who you are, without a "supporting cast"? You need to learn how to perform solo with complete confidence before you join an ensemble.

Don't get me wrong. I believe that all of us need people in our lives to help us get where we want to go, but they are only there to support us, not to determine who we are. It is not the people who support us who validate us, but the God who created us.

Getting to know yourself calls for complete and open honesty, without embarrassment or denial. Come to grips with who and what you are, and allow God to help you see yourself as He sees you. Since the One who created you is perfect, how could you be imperfect? Of course, sin has corrupted that perfection in all of us, but the new birth in Christ gives us a new nature that within itself is just as perfect as what Adam received when he was created. There is also the added challenge of being born into a world where we are forced to confront negative and hostile conditions and, quite often, an extremely dysfunctional environment.

> *...allow God to help you see yourself as He sees you.*

These things have the potential to throw us off balance and leave us spinning in the brain world of uncertainty. Don't sweat it, however. Own up to your stuff, even if it doesn't smell like an expensive fragrance from a perfume boutique in Miami Beach's BAL Harbor. You are who you are, regardless of how you got there. If you are not happy with something about yourself, don't complain...*change!* Just make sure that you are changing for yourself and not for somebody else.

No matter what you discover about yourself, remember that that you are neither a mistake nor a misfit, waiting for someone to come by and restore you. You are wonderful in your own unique way, because nobody can beat you at being you. The next time somebody challenges you to a competitive battle, ask him or her to let you pick the drill. Then tell that person, "I bet you can't beat me at being me!"

Spend some quiet time alone, just you and God, in prayer and meditation. Study the Word of God regularly, and learn just how highly He thinks of you. Positive self-help books may also be useful in developing good and healthy life principles for living. Use care and discernment in your choices, however. Make sure that you know where the author is coming from with regard to his world-view and life philosophy. Many self-help books are written from a worldly perspective, and will not help you get where you want to go.

Until you reach the place where you feel confident with who you are, until you feel "comfortable in your own skin," so to speak, it might be wise for you to thin out the crowd in your life, so that you can make more room for yourself while you're in transition. Let me suggest that you keep a journal of your thoughts and mood swings, for they can tell you a lot about yourself, as well as help you avoid denial. Once you write down the truth about yourself and your attitude, you can then reference your journal to see what you are really like, and decide if you need to make a change. If God kept a journal of His acts and ways, inspired men to write it down, called others to proclaim it, and encouraged all of us to read it so we could know Him, don't you think keeping a journal of your thoughts and feelings might help you come to know yourself better?

Another helpful exercise is to research your family history. Learning about your forebears may shed some light on some of the mysteries that exist within your personality and individuality. Before you can know where you're going, you must first know where you've been and whom you come from. Do not be shocked or ashamed when you discover certain truths about yourself; remember that everyone is perfectly made, but no one is perfect. Learn to appreciate all the good things about yourself, and to be honest about the bad things. Good and bad both combine to make you who you are.

Good and bad both combine to make you who you are.

Never, during this time of transition or at any other time, determine who you are by the standards of another person. Measure yourself and treasure yourself according to the standards by which you were created and born. I believe in role models, but those who model the role need to be clear and honest with those who follow their stars, but are not aware of their scars. This is why I always try very hard to "keep it real" in my public presentation of who I am, because I do not want to give people a false impression of myself. Then, when sin or error or imperfection inevitably shows up in my life, they will at least be able to say, "He told us so." A very dear friend of mine said something once that I thought was very real and pointed. He said, "I am too flawed to be flashy." The reality behind his statement is that we are who we are by the grace of God, and that truth should always create within us a spirit of humility that cancels out all potential and possible arrogance.

To be perfectly honest, I believe that one of the biggest errors of the church is that it has presented itself to the world as perfect, like God, rather than presenting God Himself to the world as the only perfect one. The church is so noisy in its condemnation of those who sin, but quiet in its presentation that God Himself is a forgiver and restorer of those who fall. We are so hypocritical when it comes to the imperfection of human beings, judging them not by the standards of God's compassion, mercy, and love, but by humanistic and religious theological views that originated in the mind of man. So much of what we call the "truth" is often little more than watered-down gospel and self-inflated opinions. God alone is Judge, and we must allow Him to judge His people in His time. We have our hands full trying to learn to be forgiving and merciful towards other humans who, like we, struggle day to day with unresolved issues.

Let's be honest, my spiritual brothers and sisters: we all struggle with something. I know I do. I'm not a picture of a finished product, yet, and neither are you. Don't allow yourself to be derailed when you discover some alarming and distasteful things about your personality; there is always room and time to change. Rather than getting depressed and despondent because you discovered a spot in your character, save your energy for the party you will throw for yourself once you achieve your breakthrough. Oh, and be sure to invite the entire "nay-sayers association," so that they can see what you did in your life, with God's help.

Now that you are on the road to a whole new awareness and acceptance of who you are, I want to let you in on a little secret: before long you will find yourself making progress beyond what your wildest imagination would have conceived not long ago. When you go out on a date, the person you are with gets to see the real you, confident and self-assured, not some fictitious character that you created for the purpose of being accepted. So take a deep breath and relax; it's all right to know who you are with confidence and clear certainty.

While writing this chapter, I received a poetic inspiration and jotted down the following poem about self-identity:

WHO AM I?

Who am I when I am by myself?
I am me, that's who I be.

A person with a unique and individual style,
so happy with me that I make myself smile.

I've tried to be what others would have me to be,
but I found it so hard being someone other than me.

Sure, I'd like to be accepted to avoid being alone,
but if it means that I can't be me, then I'll just be on my own.

So I'm not mad at you if you don't want me around,
just rest assured I won't let it pull me down.

You see, I've come to the knowledge of what it takes to be free;
it's not changing who I am, but accepting me for me.

You see, when God made me, He threw up His hands, and said;
I've done this once, I ain't doing it again.

So now don't you go trying to be an imitation of me;
just find out who you are and just be who you be.

Before we continue, I need to post an advance warning to those of you who are married, as well as those of you who are seeking marriage: **"PROCEED WITH CAUTION: CONFRONTATION REQUIRED."** The discussion that follows in the remainder of this chapter could be dangerous to your relationship, causing you to make some emergency changes to your present way of thinking. No longer will you be able to run from the truth of an unfulfilled marriage and a potential life filled with impossibilities, because the subjects in question are not healed, they're just hiding. Tucked inside of them is a need that has never been met and a void that has never been filled, because Momma said, "Don't tell nobody. Your issues are your issues, and what goes on in the dark stays in the dark."

The time to "come clean" is before the marriage begins.

That's fine if you plan on living by yourself for the rest of your life. But if you plan on being happy with someone, then it's better to cough it up before the wedding so that you don't choke on it later. The two of you need to sit down together and say to each other, "Tell me who you are so that I can know what I'm getting." Be open and honest in your responses. The time to "come clean" is *before* the marriage begins. Inspect now so that you can know what to expect later. If the truth about who you are and what your needs are frightens a person away from you, then that person was not equipped to handle you, nor were they deserving of you.

So often, I hear people say things like, "I'll keep it to myself; I don't want to scare anyone away," or, "I'll get over it." Will you? Don't be too sure.

CAN I REALLY CHANGE?

Anyone who says change is easy has never tried it. Change is hard, especially if you have spent years trying to fit into someone else's mold or meet someone else's expectations. Inevitably, you end up with a distorted view of who you are as a person. Stop trying to fit into something you are not cut out for. If you are a size 16, stop trying to squeeze into that pair of size 10 jeans! All you will accomplish is to cut off your circulation and leave yourself miserably uncomfortable. The solution is simple: take those jeans off and get into the size that fits who you are.

I want to propose a question to those of you for whom the pressure of trying to be perfect has left you so vulnerable that your lofty dreams of happiness and fulfillment are sinking fast into the quicksand of a disappointed life: "What do you do when the solution to your problem is not in changing who you are, but rather in *being* who you are?" This may sound simple in principle, but it is difficult in practice. Why? For one thing, you have spent all your time learning how not to be you, and now you have to regroup and try to remember who you were before you started pretending. I'm certainly not Dr. Phil, but I can tell you this much: it is going to take a persistent psychological effort on your part to pull yourself together and get rid of this pretentious person you have become.

Not everything about us can be changed; some things we just have to leave alone. I know that is a controversial statement in our modern era where everything is about image, even if it means being an imposter. Billions of dollars are spent every year in the United States alone, just on cosmetic restructuring. I have nothing against cosmetic enhancement as long as the patient has chosen to make the changes for personal fulfillment. The pressure to please someone else is never a valid reason for a person to undergo the ordeal of physical alterations of any kind. Altercation doesn't mean alteration.

Many people today are in abusive relationships and don't even know it.

Many people today are in abusive relationships and don't even know it. Any kind of manipulated pressure that is applied to a person to cause that person to act contrary to his or her will and desire, is a form of abuse. And the perpetuation of this kind of abuse has done more damage than physical abuse because it is excused simply because it is not visible. However, it destroys the self-value and self-esteem of its victims.

As a man of faith with a biblical and spiritual foundation, I must declare on the authority of God's word that any attempt to destroy the fabric of a person's individuality and sense of self-worth, whether purposely or otherwise, stands in complete opposition to the Spirit and nature of God as He is revealed in Scripture. True, God is King and Ruler of the universe and everything in it, but He is neither abusive nor coercive. And His love is unconditional, with no strings attached. How do I know this? I know from personal experience that it is the grace of God that forbears me while I myself am in transition. He has never abandoned me when I did not measure up to the standards that He set for me—and I know He never will.

I have a saying, "I can never measure up until I am allowed to grow up." Set yourself free from the bondage of people who put force *on* you but who have no faith *in* you. When God brought Eve to Adam as his helpmeet, Adam did not try to change her; he embraced her, educated her to the things of the garden, and taught her the things of God. Even when he tried to blame her when he was under pressure from God over their sin, Adam stayed the course and loved Eve beyond her shortcomings.

When I said earlier that not everything about us *can* change, I meant exactly that. Let me challenge you to come into the world of realism, the place where there is no makeup, where everybody is cool with everybody being different from each other, and where you don't hear a lot of, "Excuse me, I'm sorry I'm this size. I'll just stand over here out of everybody's way. Do you like how this looks on me? Do you like my hair? Do you think she's right for me? Is my hair too short? Does my voice sound funny? Is my nose too big? Am I too quiet? Am I too loud? Are my feet too big?"

Many times, people will try to mold and shape you according to their personal opinions and preferences. They act as though we all live in a perfect world, when the reality is that the whole world is jacked up in some way or another, not to mention all the people on it. At the same time, however, there is great beauty in the diversity of people and personalities in the world.

Ask yourself this question (and be honest): if everybody in the world were like you, what kind of world would this be? Strange doesn't mean change; oftentimes all it takes is a little explanation of who you are to the person or persons you are in relationship with. The late, great R&B maestro of love, Mr. Barry White, said it like this in brief: "Don't go changing, trying to please me...I love you just the way you are." People who really love you will not require you to change in order to meet their standard or approval. On the contrary, they will accept you for who you are and support you in the changes you want to make for your own sake.

As a Christian, I believe in miracles, but I also believe that a miracle is needed only when the situation is beyond human intervention and power, and the subject at hand is marred by some unfortunate occurrence in life. When God created you and made you different from everyone else, that was a miracle in and of itself. So here's the question: does the miracle need a miracle? Of course not. Leave it alone and let it be; you are just a piece of an eternal puzzle that God is putting together to bring glory out of the imperfect.

Change is necessary only when your behavior becomes offensive, unhealthy, immoral, ungodly, life-threatening or an endangerment to others around you. Other than these, embrace who you are and celebrate the fact that you are more than a conqueror. You are not a mistake, but rather a well-thought-out plan to bring ultimate glory to God and blessings to those who will appreciate you for being who you are. So get out from under the pressure, look at yourself in the mirror of truth, and say to the next person that tries to change you into something you're not: "I swear to tell the truth, the whole truth, and nothing but the truth, so help me God. You go and get a life, because I love who I am."

Here is another of my inspirational poems that was birthed while I was writing this chapter:

DON'T GO CHANGING

Don't spend all of your life trying to make a change

Just because people laugh at you and say that you are strange.

Don't you listen, because that ain't nothing but pumped-up hype,

Because God didn't make you to be everybody's type.

Now you've got your own little style and individuality;

You've got what God gave everybody, and that's your own personality.

So stop moping and crying and thinking that everything is wrong;

Have confidence and conviction and stand up and be strong.

People in this world are going to always have something to say,

Especially about the things that they don't understand anyway.

So you might as well hold your head up and keep looking towards the sky,

Because you're going to be who you are until it's your time to die.

A PRAYER

Father, thank You for Your undeniable love that is so consistent with Your nature. The more I live and grow, the more enlightened I am to the truth of how much You really love your people. We bless You for giving us, Your children, the opportunity to be who we are even as we try to live out Your purpose and plan for our lives. Let not the pressure of religious ridicule handicap us from experiencing the truth of Your patience and forbearing love. Bless those who believe and receive, and show mercy upon those who would criticize out of ignorance. All praise, glory, and honor to You, Father, forever. Amen.

CHAPTER FIVE

What A Man Needs

————◦◦◦————

A need is defined as something required by an individual to avoid living a life of incompleteness. Essentially, a need is a necessary thing, something we can't live without; not a life of quality, anyway. The problem in the lives of most men is not the things that we have to live with, but rather the things that we are forced to live without. It is these unmet needs, whether genuine or perceived, that lead to frustration in a relationship. Many men today chafe under the burden of a relationship that has taken a turn in the opposite direction from what would satisfy their own personal desires and needs.

Different men have different needs. There will always be people who will try to push onto us a misguided, "one-size-fits-all" standard of laws and precepts for male behavior that is based on their particular psychological and philosophical interpretations of the "do's and don'ts" of a man's life. Here is what I have to say to them: until you live in my world and in the reality of my human experiences, do not attempt to analyze me through the windows of your own personal experiences and relational encounters. Every man ought to know what he needs and should be respected for whatever his needs may be.

Honest dialogue about needs is the great missing factor in many relationships today, and a major reason why so many relationships are in trouble. Careful observation reveals that in many marriages, pretense has become the normal prescription for survival. Men and women have different needs, but often find it very difficult to define and explain those needs to each other.

Why this is the case, is really hard to say. I certainly do not have all the answers, but I hope in this chapter to explore some possible solutions, based on my personal and professional experiences, that will help couples break the silence and start talking to each other about their needs. Lack of communication, with its subsequent lack of fulfillment, is destroying marriages and families that would otherwise survive with proper guidance and positive sup-

In marriage, needs must be met, but in the single life, needs must be managed.

port. The needs of the man make up only one part of this complex issue, but that is where we will begin. We will discuss the other part of the issue, the needs of the woman, in the next chapter. Perhaps in some miraculous way these two roads will intersect with each other and create a bond of unity, honesty, openness, and passion that will ignite (or re-ignite) the fires of

love and romance in marriages that have become stale due to unrecognized, and therefore unmet, needs.

Let me urge those of you who are single not to pass over this chapter, even though it focuses on married couples. You will find some valuable truths here that will help you in your own preparations for the day when you begin sharing your life with someone. As far as needs go, my philosophy is this: In marriage, needs must be met, but in the single life, needs must be managed.

In this chapter, we will examine a profile of the different aspects of a man as they relate to his nature and his needs. Through this approach it is my intent to remove many of the mythical, misinformed, and stereotypical mental images in the minds of many, particularly women, concerning this strange and mysterious creature called, "a man." The very facts that he was created by God and was created first, are indicative of his innate value and worth. We will examine the needs of a man by considering three aspects of his nature:

1. The Created Man

2. The Relational Man

3. The Complex Man

These discussions are designed to help take some of the heat off of the often verbally battered man. The male of the human species has taken a real beating in recent years, some of it deserved, but much of it undeserved. So much emphasis has been placed on the role and importance of the woman, and what the world would be like without her, that the role of the man often has been pushed to the background. Certainly, the woman is indispensable, but so is the man. After all, it is the man who carries the seed that creates human life. Both sexes are needed, and both are often misunderstood. So let's examine some psychological, sociological, sexological, economical, and spiritual aspects, that we may better understand this creature called "man."

THE CREATED MAN

In the beginning, God created man in His own image and likeness (Gen. 1:27). He created him from the dust of the earth, breathed the Spirit of life into him, and brought man to life (Gen. 2:7). Everything that Adam was, God made him, and everything that Adam had, God gave him. Everything that Adam knew, God taught him, and every passion that Adam had, God placed within him. God placed Adam in the Garden of Eden and made him its caretaker.

In Adam, as the first three chapters of Genesis reveal him, we can see not only the image and likeness of God, but also a pre-pattern, or prototype, of potential character and likeness for every human being who was yet to be born. Adam had it all: favor and fellowship with God, his Creator; material prosperity and abundance; female companionship; and meaningful work to do. Later on, after the disaster with the serpent, he had faults and failures that led finally to family dysfunction.

Nevertheless, out of all of these things that Adam experienced, whether successes or failures, his Creator God still loved him and understood him even though discipline and judgment were necessary. Discipline is an inevitable and indispensable part of the growth process that we all must submit to if we are to become the people God has ordained us to be. We must never run from nor resist the disciplines of Almighty God, who always acts as a benevolent and loving Father toward His children. Because God loves us, He disciplines us with the same love by which He created us. He knows what is necessary for us to become all that He wants us to become. Therefore, God disciplines us in order to develop us. His purpose is to conform us to His likeness, so that we become a reflection of Him before the world that will bring glory and honor to His name.

When healthy and godly principles are followed, success is a given.

I do not believe that every man will be successful, but I do believe that every man was born to succeed and has the potential to succeed. The problem is that some men simply will not adhere to the standards and positive principles necessary to guarantee success. Everybody wants to succeed, but not everyone is willing to make the necessary sacrifices or undergo the necessary disciplines that it will take to get there. When healthy and godly principles are followed, however, success is a given.

Every man is born with the capacity to be taught and trained to become a person of character, integrity, and creativity. Personally, I believe that all men are born with a destiny to have an ingenious mind and the ability to foster into this world that which is positive and productive. That was God's original plan and design. Unfortunately, because we live in a fallen world, some males are born with birth defects or genetic or mental deficiencies that limit their growth and productivity. While exposure and environment certainly play a big part in the development of the male personality, every man has within himself the ability and the power to rise above all negative exposures and experiences.

It won't just happen. In order to become someone different, you have to *want* to become someone different. You will never become a man of good character and high integrity until you desire those traits strongly enough to undergo the discipline and to make the sacrifices necessary. There is a thing called "effort," which, when applied, can bring about favorable results in your life. You will only ever be as much as you strive to be. If you are satisfied with doing and being nothing all your life, that's your choice, pathetic though it is. On the other hand, if you put forth the effort to be a productive and successful man, you will be just that. Remember, you get out of this life whatever you put into it. Nothing just "comes" to you; even if it did, you still would have to work hard to maintain it and hold onto it. After all, "Nothing comes to a sleeper but a dream," and, "nothing comes to a lazy man but leftovers."

God's creation of man was His investment in man; therefore He made him to produce and to progress. It is only the dictates of a negative influence that cause a man to think otherwise. Negative thinking is not the created nature of man; it is born out of his inherent nature or his environmental influences. Everyone who has a negative attitude and/or behavior was taught them; they were not born with them. It is not in the sovereign nature of God to create anything or anyone with a deficiency that would cause them to be unable to succeed.

Don't get me wrong. I understand and agree with the theology of man as it relates to his fall in the garden, and that as a result of that fall sin entered into the world and became a part of man's human nature. However, I believe also in what I call the "two wills" theory of God, which says that God has two wills: His Desired will, and His Determined will. God *desires* that all men would be saved and walk in their divine purpose, but He has *determined* that not all will do so, because of their freedom of choice. God does not impose His will on anyone. We choose to believe or not believe; to obey or disobey.

There is so much we could say about the created man, but the most important thing, in the context of this book, is that man was created a whole and complete being with a divine purpose. God's desired will is that every man fulfill his ultimate purpose, experience profound blessings, and be a blessing to all those around him.

THE RELATIONAL MAN

In his original created state, man enjoyed full fellowship with God through a completely open relationship with God. Man was created to be a relational being. Even a casual look into the first few chapters of Genesis reveals the manner in which Adam related to his environment and to his God. His ability to complete his tasks as caretaker of the garden depended on his understanding of everything that was there. For example, Adam had to relate to the garden's vegetation in order to promote its growth and abundant fruitfulness as God desired. It is interesting to note in Genesis 2:5 that there was no vegetative growth until after God put Adam in the garden to nurture it and to care for it.

Not only did Adam have to relate to the vegetation in the garden, but he also had to relate to its animal life. Upon putting Adam in the garden, God gave him the assignment of naming all the animals (Gen. 2:19-20). Adam had to understand the natures of each of the animals in order to know how to give oversight to them.

In order to relate to something or someone, you must study it and know it.

The same is true today with any kind of relationship. In order to relate to something or someone, you must study it and know it. Your power to influence persons or events depends on the level of your knowledge and understanding. Men who do not sharpen their skills will always be shy and fall short in pursuit of their purpose.

I know men who pretend to be knowledgeable of something in order to protect the position of their ego and self-conceit, and will allow that thing to fail before they admit that they do not know what they are doing. Many of us men need to alter our egos before we end up losing everything we have. Why do we find it so hard to admit when we don't know something? Our ego trips us up. Acknowledging ignorance on a particular matter does not diminish our manhood. In fact, it takes a strong man of character and integrity to humble himself and say, "I don't know, but I'm willing to learn."

One of the reasons that men are so often misunderstood is because many of us have lost much of our ability to be relational effectively, especially with women (including our wives) and our children. This is due in part to our culture, which holds in high esteem the strong, independent, self-made man who relies (and therefore relates) to no one. Other factors could include family upbringing, lack of knowledge based upon lack of teaching, absence of positive male role models, insecurities, exposure to abuse, fear of failure, misguided information, and intimidation. The biggest reason, however, is the sin nature we inherited from Adam. Our natural relational ability has been distorted by sin. Many of us are good at our vocational and recreational pursuits, but have a very difficult time in other important areas.

Closely linked to our relational problems is difficulty in communication. In my experience, I have noted that one of the most frustrating things to women regarding men is our inability or unwillingness to communicate with them, especially when they see us communicating just fine with the other guys. The problem usually is not that we are not good communicators, but that we do not communicate in the same way that women communicate. Women can seem a bit pushy sometimes because they try to understand men through the eyes of their female creative natures.

A WORD TO THE LADIES

Ladies, if you really want to understand the man in your life, you have to see him as he is and work with him on that level. Men generally are task-oriented, territorial, and less transparent than you because we have a protective nature that causes us to be defensive about our positions. Even though we may not be able to explain it, we just go straight to the point on an issue to avoid excessive dialogue or debate. Oftentimes we become aggressively defensive as our way of telling you to back off, because you are making us feel intimidated and as though we are under interrogation.

Is this fair to you, ladies? Perhaps not, but there is a way to get the lion to lie down with the lamb, a way to get the beast to behave, a way to get him to respond to you with genuine communication. One of the first rules for getting a man to communicate is to talk not *at* him or *down to* him, but to talk *to* him in a tone and manner that allow him to feel respected at all points of the conversation. Oftentimes, the rush to get to the issue at hand takes precedence over the manner in which the issue is presented. Remember, "Presentation takes priority over the point being pushed." Any time a man feels that his woman is attacking him, he will become defensive.

Ladies, let me urge you to develop a personal strategy of communicational manipulation so that you can get your men to talk. You have to use the power of your femininity (not your sexuality) to get him to feel comfortable and safe when talking to you. He must never feel as though you are trying to lead him, but find a way to make him feel as though he is still respected by you and seen as the leader in the relationship. Don't ask me to tell you how to do that, because every man is different and every situation is different. Use your own creative knowledge and power to develop a personalized plan for your personalized man. And remember, never allow your personality to interfere with the issue. Get past your personality, humble yourself in the situation, and deal with the issue at hand. Success is much more likely if both of you speak and behave respectfully toward each other.

Due to the lack of available information and resource groups in our families, churches and communities, we men often have to go on our instinct when it comes to relationships. We are products of our environment and cannot excel any higher than our own personal exposures. Most men will never go any farther than they have already gone, because they fear failure. Society has taught us that as men we must always have it together because so many other lives depend upon us.

However true this may be, such a burden of responsibility creates within many men a fear of stepping out of the box, therefore limiting their potential and locking them into a system that is not very male-friendly. Men must be given the room to err as they strive to maximize their potential by minimizing their personal insecurities. Every man has the God-given ability to be at the head of his game and to gain good ground in the area of his personal success. He must, however, be allowed to follow his passion and his vision, in which lie the power to produce purpose.

Sisters, please cut the brothers some slack, and understand that you cannot program them into being what you want them to be. They have already been pre-programmed by their Creator, and your interference is just that—interference. Support his dreams and offer him your support, even if he does not ask you for it. This will encourage him, because then he knows you care. Don't try to tell him what to do, but feel free to offer suggestions. For example, never say, "You should do this or that." Say instead, "Have you ever thought about doing it this way?" Using this approach both supports him and causes him to feel as though he is in control of his situation.

Support his dreams and offer him your support, even if he does not ask you for it.

Men are driven by their ego, and a healthy ego can be an enhancing tool for a man's progress. Whatever you do, ladies, do not attack or defame your man's ego. Remember that, "Wherever his ego's, he goes." Learn to build up his confidence through encouragement and positive exhortation. Every woman has the ability to be both constructive and destructive, so choose the road of wisdom, as expressed by King Solomon: "A wise woman builds her house; a foolish woman tears hers down with her own hands" (Prov. 14:1, NLT).

Tradition says that men generally are not very relational beings, and public discussion in our culture has tended to reinforce this view. I submit to you that this is a false and flawed picture. We men may be guilty of many things, but being non-relational is not one of them. On that issue, among others, we have often been found guilty as charged, but without a fair trial. Let's examine the evidence. Sometimes the evidence against us is very prejudicial and purely circumstantial. Sometimes a judgment is made based on nothing more substantial than an impression or an assumption. An all-female jury leaves plenty of room for an unfair trial. Women look at a man's tough exterior and often jump to the conclusion that the way he appears on the outside is the way he is on the inside.

Ladies, when you are trying to understand your men, take time to interview the source. Listen to our hearts and you will know that we have emotions and feelings. We hurt, even though we may not say anything; that's just our way of coping with our fights, faults, and failures. We have to encourage ourselves even when no one else does. Sometimes this can cause us to become vulnerable to so many things that are outside of the created will of God.

I am not trying to make excuses for our sometimes confusing or irritating behavior, because I know some of the stuff we deal with we have brought on ourselves. Some men simply are set in their ways, trapped by their own bad habits, feeding on a diet of self-imposed will and seasoned stubbornness. These are the kinds of men who know that their self-imposed will is causing them to become emotionally nauseated, resulting in excessive vomiting of negative behavior. But to save face and their delicate ego, they privately eat their own vomit in order to avoid public shame and acknowledgement that they are "jacked up" in some areas of their lives and need to make some modifications and adjustments in their character.

Unfortunately, I am not equipped to provide all the information on this subject, but I can give personal testimony to the fact that men are very relational beings. As far as the man/woman relationship, it takes the right woman—a true woman—to bring out a man's best qualities, those traits that will help him excel and become all he can be. In the Genesis creation narratives, when the serpent decided to get man to go against the law of God and eat of the forbidden tree, he knew that he could never influence man directly to disobey God. So what did he do? He went to the one who alone had the ability to influence Adam to move beyond his God-given restriction: the woman, Adam's wife. Through the power of her created femininity, Eve got Adam to do what Satan himself could not get him to do.

So ladies, don't be hard or defeated. Be woman: soft, sensitive, sensuous, strategic, spiritual, sexy, sweet, and strong. Concentrate on building up your man instead of breaking him down and leaving him feeling worthless. Teach him what he doesn't know. Sweet-talk him into where you want him to go. Remind the men in your life, whether husband, father, brother, son, fiancé, or friend, that they are kings fit for a kingdom and destined to rule in power and authority. Don't write us off before you get to know us and see us for who we really are.

Here is another poem that came to me while I was writing this chapter. It's all about understanding men.

GETTING TO KNOW ME

Get to know me and you'll understand
The struggles I face in being a man.
The change, the challenges, the hurt, and the pain,
When you try to do your best, but you're making no gain.
Now look deep inside of me, my sister, and say what you see,
I bet you didn't even know that I had all of that within me.
For there is so much more to being a man,
Than the size of the thing that's inside of his pants.
A man must be smart and wise and think on his feet,

He must major in brains and minor in sheets.

You see, all men are not dogs, like women often say,

You just picked the wrong one, and let the right one get away.

So give a brother a break and an encouraging word,

And don't judge me on rumors and gossip you've heard.

Get to know me first, and then you'll see,

That I am a man of heart and pure quality.

RESPONSIBILITY: WHO'S TO BLAME?

One sign of immaturity is the unwillingness to take on responsibility, especially when the person so refusing is the one upon whom everything depends. Men are to be responsible in every positive way, meeting their assignments head-on, even if it requires some confrontation. Whenever we do not handle our business, it goes undone, and the responsibility falls upon someone else, often someone who is neither equipped nor positioned to handle it. Now someone has to do double duty because some brother did not handle his assignment.

As men, we must be prepared at all times to give leadership in our homes, churches, communities, and workplaces. Many hardships, problems, and failures could be avoided if more of us men would simply shoulder our legitimate responsibility rather than trying to shift it (and the blame for failure) onto someone else.

In all fairness, however, before a man can be expected to assume responsibility of any sort, he must be made fully aware of what is being asked of him, so that nothing takes him by surprise. Most men do not like to be given responsibility for something without first being thoroughly informed on every aspect of the assignment.

A man's ability to assume responsibility does not suddenly appear when he becomes an adult, but must be nurtured while he is still a boy. Fathers and mothers, teach your boys how to be responsible, so that when they become men they will know what responsibility is all about. Teach them how to take care of themselves. Teach them how to cook, clean house, wash, dry, and iron their clothes, make up their own beds, balance their checkbooks, and save their money. Teach them how to treat a woman, how to be gentlemen, and how to be gentle. Teach them that they are not supposed to run around town making babies and populating the earth with their seed and raising the statistics on single-family homes and sexually transmitted diseases. These things must be taught while they are still boys, so that they will grow into mature, responsible men.

When things go wrong, real men do not look for excuses or ways to blame others; if they are responsible, they step up to the plate and say so. Real men do not leave others holding the bag for their own mistakes. Personally, I believe that most of the problems and challenges that face our world and our families are due to the lack of male responsibility. I hear so many men say that they are not in a position in society to be effective. To those men I would say: "Don't believe it. Work from wherever you are with whatever you have. You do not need recognition or position; you need responsibility and passion. Therein lies your power to influence your environment and to cause positive things to happen in your life and in the lives of those around you."

We do not fail when we make mistakes; we fail when we do not learn from them.

Many men try to pass the blame off on someone else because they erroneously believe that one mistake makes them a failure. Everybody makes mistakes because nobody's perfect. Men, think how peaceful our hearts would be if we could simply accept the fact that we're going to make mistakes and that it's okay to do so! We do not fail when we make mistakes; we fail when we do not learn from them.

A champion boxer does not quit once he loses a fight. Instead, he trains even harder and challenges the person who beat him to a rematch. In the light- heavyweight fight between Antonio Tarver and Bernard Hopkins, two fighters that I admire very much, the first fight between them went all twelve rounds, with Tarver remaining the champion. He was the better fighter, and in better condition than the aging, forty-year-old Hopkins. Many said that Hopkins should simply retire and give up his quest for the light-heavyweight championship. Hopkins, however, did not listen to the opinions of others, and got his rematch. He went into intense training and conditioning, and in the next fight he went twelve rounds, this time with different results: he took the title from Tarver. Tarver made this observation: "Hopkins was better conditioned for the fight, so he deserved the win."

I believe that every man seeking success in this life must develop for himself a no-excuse policy. Blaming others is not a mature way of handling our business. We have to always be in control of who we are and what we do. That means we need to stop saying things like, "So-and-so made me do it." When we say that, we are admitting that something or someone else has more control and influence over our life than we do. To me, that is worse than blaming someone else.

We must always be on guard, relative to what we allow to influence us. All of us have been given personal assignments to accomplish in life, and we must take personal responsibility to guard that which has been given into our trust and care. Taking personal responsibility means being willing to do whatever is necessary to protect those under our care from injury or harm, even if it means dying for them. There is neither honor nor dignity in blaming others for our failures.

In Genesis 3:8-17, we see the blame game in full play. When God made His normal visit to the garden to fellowship with His children, He did not find

Adam in his normal place or posture. God called out to Adam, not because He could not locate him, but rather to get Adam to respond on his own. He said, "Adam, where are you?" In other words, "What is your state of mind?" Adam responded by saying, "I heard you coming, and hid myself, because I was naked." That's what sin does: it uncovers us and shows us things about ourselves that we did not know existed, and that we don't want others to see.

God then asked Adam a very unveiling question: "Who told you that you were naked? Have you eaten the fruit that I told you not to eat?" Adam replied, "Yes, but it was the woman that you gave me who brought me the fruit." (Blame game alert!) Then God asked the woman, "How could you do such a thing?" "The serpent tricked me," she answered. (Blame game alert!) When confronted with their sin, Adam and Eve each blamed somebody else and refused to accept responsibility for their own actions.

Both already had clear instructions on this matter. It would have been better for Adam to assume the responsibility, because he was given the leadership role in the garden, and should not have listened to his wife (in this instance, anyway). Men have the God-given role of leader in their families. It is our responsibility to ensure that there is a clear vision, and that everyone in the home understands and follows that vision without detour. And if anything happens within that family that threatens that vision, we need to be man enough to confront it and correct it with tender loving care. It does not matter who set the house on fire; if no direction is given, everyone will burn up.

Here is a poem I wrote to inspire us as men to step to the plate and accept responsibility for those God has placed in our charge:

A CHARGE TO KEEP

You've been given a charge, you've been given a plan,
You must assume responsibility and act like a real man.
There's no time for relaxing, No time for being still,

You must work real hard for you have a charge to fulfill.

If things go wrong, and they sometimes will,

You must not pass the blame; you should rather be killed.

It's not always easy being a man;

There is a lot of responsibility that falls in your hand.

But don't run from the challenges that you will face everyday;

Just remember you have a charge to keep, and whatever you do, don't walk away.

THE COMPLEX MAN

Believe it or not, men are complex creatures. The areas of a man's complexity that I feel are most often confusing to women in relating to him are his communication skills, his competence, and his confidence. All these are so closely knitted together in a man's make up that he needs to excel in all of these areas in order to excel in any of them. I am not a psychologist by profession, and therefore I will not attempt to give a psychological analysis of the thought patterns of men. On the other hand, I am a man with a lot of professional and personal experience dealing with men. My goal here is to both agree with and explain some of the claims that women have as they relate to men. However, our exploration will be from the male perspective.

As I expressed earlier, when it comes to understanding and relating to men, unless you *are* a man, all you have is interpretation, not revelation. I could give you my interpretation of the behavior of a gorilla, gained through patterns of research and study, but if the gorilla could speak for himself, I am sure he would reveal things about his thought patterns and behavior that would blow our minds and research out of the water. Remember also that no one person has all the answers on any one subject. I make no claim to being the brainiest on this subject, so I will try to keep it real, based on my own personal feelings, views, and experiences.

COMMUNICATION

Why is it so hard for men to communicate? That is a question filled with a whole lot of egocentric answers. It is not that men do not know how to communicate, but that we like to determine when we communicate, with whom we communicate, and how we communicate. Men, let's admit it: women are better communicators than we are. We may be more direct in our communication, but women are more descriptive and detailed.

Ladies, when communicating with a man, especially if it is going to be an intense conversation that will require him to answer a lot of questions or explain a decision he made, you must follow a careful strategy. He must never feel as though he is being challenged, because his male nature is pre-programmed to protect his position. Ask your questions in such a way that he will not feel threatened by them.

I imagine that some of you females may think this is childish and unnecessary. It isn't; not if you want to get your questions answered. Having a strategy to get your man to communicate with you is crucial. I know of lawyers who will spend countless hours researching and planning their strategy before asking one question of a witness in a court trial. If your relationship with your man is important to you, then you are going to have to learn how he functions.

Remember, love is never puffed up, and it does not seek its own way. Therefore, it is important to know what calms your man, as well as what sets him off, so you can plan how to present your questions and concerns without putting him in a defensive mode. Always use a loving approach. Never tell him that he does not know how to communicate, but speak in a manner that will make him feel as though you are helping in this area, so that he can represent your family and himself well at all times.

Even if your primary goal is to get him to communicate with you, don't make it obvious that this is what you're doing; otherwise, he will feel that you are trying to get over on him, or weaken him, and that definitely will not help your relationship. Try to observe how he communicates with his buddies, and use those same tactics. Remember that the issue is not the issue, but how the issue is presented. Learn his personality, develop your plan around his personality, and use your plan to get him to talk.

Another important thing to keep in mind is that timing is everything. Know your man's mood swings and watch his mood; you will know because he wants you to know what mood he is in. Unlike most women, men generally are very predictable. Their moods are usually easy to read. Most men have a routine that they follow, and from which they rarely depart. This is why it is easy for a woman to know when her man is cheating: his patterns will change. Men do not change their patterns unless something or someone else has caught their interest. More on this in chapter nine.

I have been a public speaker since the age of nineteen, and at the age now of forty-nine, I speak before thousands of people over the course of a year. It was easy for me to assume that this much speaking experience automatically made me a good communicator. I was as wrong as wrong could be. I am a skilled public speaker by gift, but I have to work at being a skilled communicator. One of my ministry sons said that we have not communicated effectively with each other until we are both saying the same thing and have the same understanding. Just because you tell a person something does not mean you have communicated effectively and with clarity to that person.

Whenever my father told one of us to do something, he always sealed his instruction with a question: "Do you understand what I just told you?" I believe he did this to cover himself in case I, or one of my siblings, tried to use the "I did not understand" excuse for not doing what he said.

Even to this day, communicating what I want done, and how I want it done, is often a challenge, because I expect that when I give a task to someone that he or she will do it the way I would do it. I sometimes fail to realize the importance of being sure that he or she understands with clarity what

I expect. I must also avail myself to this person, in case the need arises to communicate with me regarding any other concerns or challenges he or she may have. I have also had to learn that, no matter what thoughts, plans, or ideas may be in my head, until I have spoken them to my wife with my mouth, I have failed to communicate. If I cannot recall what I told her, or when I told her, it's usually safe to assume that I did not tell her.

Effective communication is a skill all by itself, and not many men major in this area. This fact should never make a man feel weakened, however; he just needs a support system that understands him psychologically and supports him in this process. It is so important, when a man chooses a woman to spend his life with, that he does not just find someone who stimulates him sexually. Truth be told, women like that are a dime a dozen. What every man needs is a woman who will stimulate his mind. If she does not know how to communicate with him or stimulate him intellectually, he will soon become bored with her.

> *What every man needs is a woman who will stimulate his mind.*

A wife is supposed to be her husband's helpmeet, and that involves more than just domestic responsibility. It also involves helping him think out his vision for his family and future. She should know how to keep him focused and fashioned towards his purpose, not competing with him but complimenting and accommodating him.

Ladies, let me warn you in advance: if you ever try to compete with him, you will lose him. You may win the fight or the discussion; you may win the communication battle; but I guarantee that you will lose *him*, even if he never moves out. Whenever you damage his ego and cause him to feel as though you have weakened him, he will shut down as far as "you" are concerned. And remember, if he isn't talking to you, he's talking to someone. I know it may not seem so on the surface, but we men really do like to talk.

COMPETENCY AND CONFIDENCE

A man's confidence is linked to his competence. Most men, by nature, will not attempt to do something publicly without first being confident in his own mind that he will be able to do it. His confidence comes from within, not from without. A man never wants to lose; even the man who is not a sore loser still wants to win. Rest assured, if a man sets out to do something, he is confident he can do it, regardless of how stupid or idiotic it might appear. And when a man believes he can do something, he usually does it. He is driven by his ego, and once he sets his mind towards something, there is usually nothing anyone can say that will cause him to change his course.

Even though men do not like to fail, they would rather fail at something they had confidence in and knowledge of, rather than not try it at all simply because someone else said it is not a good idea. Never tell a man that his idea is not a good idea, especially when it has taken him a lot of self-effort to reach the place where he is willing to take a risk and be creative. If cautionary advice is in order, it might be better to say something like, "Maybe this is not a good idea at this time." This way he will not feel that his idea has been insulted, but that the issue is not his idea, but the timing. Not only will this preserve his confidence; it also will give him the opportunity to use wisdom along with his competent knowledge.

How much better relationships will be when couples learn the importance of edification, which is the art of building up each other. Men have their own way of thinking, and should be allowed to think for themselves without always having to give an explanation to the women in their lives for everything they do. Freedom of thought is our God-given right, and if we don't use our brains and train our brains, we will end up with no drive, no confidence, low self-esteem, no dreams, and no visions.

There are some people who feast on destroying a man's self-worth; they find it easy to tear him down in order that they may raise themselves above him. I know of women who have wonderful husbands who work hard to give them a good life, and they just hammer away at their ego and self-esteem. They humiliate them in front of their friends and family, never encouraging them, and get upset if someone else pays them a compliment. To be sure, there are men who are the same way, but we'll deal with that later.

In this competitive world we live in, where women often are more educated than men, but are still a minority in the working world, many companies will hire a woman in front of a man in order to meet their quota on minority hiring. Some men can handle competition, whereas others can't stand the pressure.

A woman can be the driving force behind her man. When no one else can get a man to do something, a woman can. If a woman asks a man in a gentle way to do something, consider it done. I can remember when, as the director of one of my productions, I had asked over and over again for some of the men of the church to volunteer as stage hands to help out during the play. I got very few responses, so I changed my strategy: I put my wife in charge of the stage. She made two appeals for the same thing, and ended up with more men than she could use, and more men than we've ever had.

Sisters, you are going to have to make the investment of building up your man in the area of his confidence. Challenge him to make himself competitive by enhancing his level of competence. Help him to understand that he can do whatever he puts his mind to. Push him, but pamper him if he fails, and encourage him to get back into the race. Make him feel that you need him to be the best he can be so that you can be the best you can be. Make sure he knows that you stand by him as a supporter of the vision. Remember that insulating him with encouragement is better than he isolating you through the silence of a bruised ego.

To the men, I say: strive hard to be the best *you* that you can be. You must invest in yourself before you can expect anyone else to invest in you. Because you are what you eat, watch what you feed your mind, body, and spirit. Feast on things that will bring positive and pure production into your life. Always remember that no one owes you anything; it is up to you to get in the race and give it your best shot. Set your goals high and strive to reach them; do not set your standards low no matter who says so.

You have been created by the infinite hand and wisdom of Almighty God. Do not allow yourself to be hindered by the critics who tell you that you will not make it because of your skin color, the community you grew up in, or the education that you do not have. I heard all of those things myself growing up, but I decided many years ago, while still a youth, that I would never allow the criticisms or the commentary of men to determine my destiny. I have lived through many mistakes and mess ups, I have survived through personal hurt and hardships, and I still hold onto the confidence that I have in the person that God made me.

Why be born an original, only to end up dying as a copy?

You have to live off of being who you are and not off of what others expect of you. Learn to use your gifts and abilities as tools for advancing your life. Be honest with yourself and don't try to be who you are not. Why be born an original, only to end up dying as a copy? Remember to work your stuff, because that's the stuff that works.

Growing up as a kid, I had a very bad speech impediment; I stammered in my speech to the point where I would stomp the floor to get my words out. Other children, some being my friends and siblings, did what kids normally do: they made fun of my speech. To be honest, if I had been somebody else, I would have laughed at me, too. The only time it really bothered me was if the girls were around and the guys made fun of me, or if I had to read in class and kids would laugh.

I was in the third grade at Alta Sita Elementary School in East St. Louis, Illinois, where I grew up. My teacher's name was Mrs. Lucille Gurdon, a very sweet lady who was a member of a church where I had been invited to sing in a program. She did not know I could sing, because I was new to her class and school, and my family was new to that community. So I get up there with this big voice coming out of this little body, and after the service was over, she came up to me in absolute amazement and said, "Where did you get all of that voice from?" I told her, "From my mother." She was so excited and so out done.

Well, I thought that was the end of it, until the following Monday. At school that day, Mrs. Gurdon, without notifying me, announced to the class that she had heard me sing, and then asked me to come in front of the class and sing a song. Back in those days, we did whatever an adult told us to do. So there I was, this stammering-speech kid, in front of a class of skeptics, spectators, and some smiling faces that had ugly written all over them. I opened my big mouth, and without a stammer or a slur amazed that class. All the little girls were screaming over my voice.

Every time I look back on that experience, the revelation is always clear to me. What Mrs. Gurdon did on that day was to call me to the front so that I could do what I was very good at. And the result? My friends and class-mates left school that day not talking about the kid who stammered when he talked, but buzzing about how that new kid, Carlos, could sing better than everybody in the school. I learned to never focus on my weaknesses, but on my strengths. And look at me now: that stammering-speech kid gets paid big time to talk to thousands of people on a weekly basis.

Life can really be funny if you keep laughing. Learn to live with who you are and don't let being a man put any unnecessary pressure on you. You are a man no matter what mistakes you make or bad roads you take. You can always take the next exit and get back on the right track, only next time, watch the signs, because they are there to guide you.

In closing, let me share another poem with a message to the sisters about the brothers:

I'M A MAN

I am a man and I have needs just like you.

I have emotions and feelings and can be sensitive too.

Sometimes I laugh, sometimes I even cry,

Sometimes I'm not so strong, no matter how hard I try.

I like to be hugged and kissed just like you do,

And told that I did a good job when my work is through.

Don't just think that I'm just tough and hard as a nail,

For my feelings do get hurt when I don't succeed, but fail.

For years I was told that real men don't cry,

Well, whoever made that up was telling a lie.

One thing that I discovered that is very real and true,

And that is being a real man has to do with what's inside of you.

So to all of the men who feel the pressure of this male life,

Go ahead, scream, and get emotional just like your girlfriend or your wife.

You're not weak when you do this, for you can still make your stand,

Because no matter how long you live, you will always be a man.

CHAPTER SIX

What A Woman Needs

(FROM A MAN'S POINT OF VIEW)

———◆———

Let me say at the outset that I am fully aware of the challenge I have undertaken with this chapter. Some might even call me presumptuous for trying it. The very idea of attempting, as a man, to assess and discuss the needs of women, may seem the height of arrogance to some, while laughably naïve to others.

But I do not approach this subject with no credentials. Having the experience of being a son to my mother, a brother to three sisters, a husband and lover to my wife of 27 years, a father to my twin daughters, and a spiritual and professional counselor to thousands of women throughout my thirty years of ministry, I believe that I have come to understand, without the persuasion of bias or a prejudicial perspective, the needs of a woman. At the same time, I readily acknowledge that, like the gorilla analogy in the last chapter, without being a woman, there is no way I can fully and completely identify with a woman's needs. That is why this chapter deals with a woman's needs *from a man's point of view*; it could be no other way.

Any man who plans to have a lifelong relationship with a woman should make it his purpose to educate himself regarding her general nature and her needs, both general and specific. General needs refer to her needs as a woman; specific needs refer to her needs as a *specific, individual woman* who is unique from all others. While women are very different in their individual personalities, they are quite similar in their created female person. (Men are the same way.)

One of the most common problems within male and female relationships is that they try to understand each other from the point of view of their own gender. This can lead quickly to confusion, because men and women think differently from each other, and usually express their needs differently. Harmony and contentment come when each person is willing to dissect the other's individuality and seek with an open mind to understand each other based on human reality rather than wishful thinking. We are who we are individually, and must never try to understand each other from an opposing or conflicting view. Men should not be expected to think like women, nor women like men. No, we must live to learn about each other and be willing to set aside our own ego and needs long enough to develop the desire to reach the other person from his or her place of need.

The power of a woman's femininity is virtually unlimited.

One of the myths of womanhood says that women, because of the unpredictability of their emotions, can never be understood by men. I disagree completely. Through discipline, desire, determination, and a little flexibility, men can come to understand anything they set their hearts and minds to understand. A man does not have to compromise who he is in order to comprehend the needs of the woman he has chosen to enter into a relationship with. All he has to do is remain concentrated on her and make sure he has plenty of patience. Along the way, he must be ready to conquer the bumps of his own "foot-in-the-mouth" kind of mistakes and get comfortable with saying, "I'm sorry," because sometimes that will be his only way to a place of peace.

A woman is a very beautiful being that God has given both to her man and to her world to cause them to become much better entities. The power of a woman's femininity is virtually unlimited. I believe that God gave them a little something extra that He didn't give us men, and I have learned to reverence and respect whatever that something is. She is too smart to let anything get by her, and even if she doesn't say anything, that is not a sign that she doesn't know anything. I have learned these valuable lessons the hard way as they relate to the importance of my wife as a woman given to me by God for the purpose of helping me to fulfill the purpose for which I was created.

Can a man make it without a woman? Can a woman make it without a man? The obvious answer to both questions is yes. But some of us were created to be united with someone with whom we find that complementary connection that creates a powerful and positive partnership. I always say that if God made anything better than a beautiful woman (meaning inner beauty of spirit), He kept it for Himself.

So fasten your seat belt and prepare yourself to journey with me into the inner circle of the psychological, emotional, sexual, intellectual, and physical world of that wondrous being we know as "woman."

On our journey we will explore many areas of concern to women that will bring some clarity and understanding of their needs when in a relationship with a man. These topics are not arranged in order of priority, for all of them are equally important to a woman in order for there to be a peaceful balance within that relationship. For the men, a word to the wise: do not treat these topics on a "choose-one-over-the-other" basis; these are not merely "wants" that women have, but needs: necessary mandates that require full attention and faithful accommodation.

With that firmly in mind, let's journey now into the world of "Sheology."

SECURITY

Being secure sits at the top of the list of most women as a major concern and need. In researching the word "secure," I found some definitions that really give a very simplistic understanding to the word. Webster defines secure as being without care or anxiety, and to be confident in expectation. Women cannot live in a situation of uncertainty; it is their human nature to need to know the direction they are headed. Women, in order to feel secure, thrive on detail. They don't like limited information. It is important to them to know clearly what they are getting themselves into.

Men have sex with their bodies; women have sex with their minds.

For most women, a spirit or feeling of insecurity will frustrate a male/female relationship faster than just about anything else. It is hard for a woman to feel or be sexy for her husband when she doesn't feel safe. In order for her mind to be free, she has to know that everything is all right. Men have sex with their bodies; women have sex with their minds, which is why when a woman has stressful things on her mind, it is hard for her to bring her body to a place of intimacy. She performs much better when her mind is free of congestive worry and concern. Some men make the terrible mistake of seeing her unresponsiveness as rejection, when in actuality it is her reaction to her creative nature, which mandates peace before pleasure, not pleasure to get peace. A woman needs to feel secure, and she needs to know that her man will not compromise in this area of need.

Some of the areas where women need to feel secure include: finances, family, and future planning. We will now examine each of these areas in turn.

FINANCES

Money is important to women, and therefore should be important to every man who plans on having a relationship with a woman. Why is money so important to women? Women in general are known to be hard workers and strong on education, knowledge, and on raising their awareness in order that they may remain competitive. This being the case, a woman needs a man who can stimulate her and challenge her in these areas by having his own game together. No real woman wants a man who cannot provide leadership in this area.

It has taken the repetition of many costly mistakes and errors for me to gain this knowledge. I have learned through painful experience that a woman would rather have a little stuff with much security than a lot of stuff with little security. Women find security not in what they have to spend, but in how much they have left *after* they have spent. Trying to manipulate around this mandate is a waste of time, because it is not going to happen.

Much of the frustration I have had in my marriage could have been dealt with easily if I had only had my money game together. My wife has never told me not to do something that I wanted to do, but she always tells me to make sure that I can afford to do it. When I hear the words, "afford to do it," I interpret it as, "Make sure that you can cover the bases in case the project doesn't do what you plan for it to do, and be prepared to deal with the consequences." That is not what she said. When she says, "Make sure you can afford it," what she means is, "If doing this is going to take away from the family's security, causing us to have to struggle and strain and worry about how we are going to pay our own personal bills, then don't do it."

There are two trains of thought on this. One has to do with faith in the vision that you believe that God has given you, and the other involves counting the cost to see if you can finish what you start. Both can be right, and both have their pros and cons. For the sake of peace in the relationship, however, you have to find a place of agreement without compromise. If you don't, your home will suddenly feel like a war zone, and your bedroom, a refrigerator. Do not put the financial security of your marriage in jeopardy; nothing is worth that.

Trust me; I had to learn this the hard way. I have enormous faith in God, but if I could change anything about the past years of my marriage, it would be to listen more to the wisdom of my wife at the same time, so that I would not become careless and deceived by my own desire to do that which I felt called to do. Why have a wife and helpmeet at all if I am not going to listen to her, especially when she is a woman of integrity? Had I listened years ago to the voice and concerns of the woman God gave to me, we would have had a better handle on the financial things that are so important to the advancement of a relationship. It took me a long time to learn that the issue is not how much money we make, but how much of that money we can keep to help us make more money.

Avoid, if possible, the person who does not have financial discipline in his or her life.

Because of my own experiences, I strongly urge each of you to hold fast to these standards and do not compromise them. Avoid, if possible, the person who does not have financial discipline in his or her life. Ladies, if your man is expecting you to follow him into marriage, check his banking skills, because that will tell you a lot about his ability to perform. I am not suggesting that a woman kick a brother to the curb simply because he is not good about managing his money, but I am saying that his wife or fiancée should help him.

To the men I say: if you do not have the discipline to create the financial security for your family that is needed, don't be stupid in your masculinity; let your wife handle this area. If she is unable to manage it, find a financial advisor who can help you stay on the right track. A paycheck is short-term, and, for most couples, is controlled by an employer. Security, however, is for a lifetime. If you are looking for a real woman, know that you are going to have to have financial security in your plan. Otherwise, you might as well start stepping on, because women thrive on financial security in their marriages or other relationships.

FAMILY SECURITY

Family is precious to a woman, and the security of her family is of paramount importance. A wife must know that her relationship with her husband is secure and that she is the highest priority in his life (next to God). No woman wants to go through life wondering if she is in competition with another woman for her husband's affection and devotion. A woman who understands femininity understands also that she has to keep her "game" up, because the male population is low, but the female population is high. Keeping a man is a competitive sport in these days and times, especially when marriage is no longer a deterrent for people looking for good companionship.

No wife should ever be made to feel that she has to compete for her husband. She should feel secure in the knowledge that she already has him. It is the husband's responsibility to do whatever is needed for her to arrive and remain at that place of security. If he doesn't, she will frustrate him no end.

No wife should ever be made to feel that she has to compete for her husband.

Men, flirt with your wives. I cannot overstress the importance of this. Compliment her. Tell her she looks good and smells good. Kiss her neck and tell her she tastes good. Tell her and show her that she means just as much to you now—and more—as she did when you first fell in love with her. Don't let sex be the motive always for your compliments and attentive interest in her. Tell her all of these things, and, at times, back off and don't even pursue her for sex. She needs to know from you that she is not just someone for you to get your sexual groove on with.

Introduce her to all of your friends, both male and female. If you work with a group of women, make sure that she knows that they know you are married and are committed to your marriage. While this may sound insignificant to some of you, it is essential for the security of your woman. It is important to her to know where you are, not because she doesn't trust you, but just in case she needs you; this is her way of feeling secure. Here's a word of wisdom to all you married men: anywhere you go that you can't take your wife or tell her about is a place you need to stop hanging around. It is perfectly normal for a woman to want to feel secure in her relationship with her man. God created her from him and for him, and she should be secured by him if she is going to be in covenant with him.

While we are on the subject of family, it is important to a woman to know how she and her mate as a couple will relate and respond to the in-law factor. She needs to feel secure in the knowledge that there will be balance and fairness in relating to both families—hers and his—and that their own family will always take precedence. A woman should never fear that her mate's family will ever come between her and him. No woman wants to be second to her husband's mother at any time, and rightfully so. Because a woman takes pride in her home, visits by in-laws or extended family should be planned in advance and not sprung on her at the last minute. This will help to avoid unnecessary tension and division that could create a very unhealthy relationship.

Physical protection is another area of security that women look for in their relationships with their men. A woman must be confident that her man would be willing to give his life for her if it came down to it. I am talking about a man literally, physically dying for her if that's what it takes to protect her. One of the things I have always done that may seem simple to many but it is significant to my wife, is that whenever we are walking, I always walk on the outside so that if a car happens to run up on the curb, I will take the hit first and be able to push her out of the way. This is one way I have of saying to her that her safety and security are more important to me than my own.

No woman wants to be with a man she feels is incapable of protecting her from physical harm. She wants to know that in the heat of battle, or if she is being hassled by someone, that her husband or male companion is going to defend her honor. And brothers, she has every right to expect that from us. It is my Christian and moral conviction that any man who cannot or will not protect his wife or female companion is not worthy of her.

Being "king of the castle" means more than giving orders and having people at your beck and call; it also means guarding with intensity the safety and security of your wife and children. It means that if she is going home ahead of you, that you call and make sure she made it in the house safely, and let her know how long she will be at home without your physical presence. This is something that every man should take pride in doing without hesitation or reservation. Whenever God gives you the most precious gift of His creation (which is woman), you should reverence her by making sure that she knows that you've got her back in any situation, even if it means putting your own life in danger.

Spiritual protection is a vital but grossly neglected area of security that all women need from the men in their lives. Too many couples do not factor into their relationships the need for spiritual protection. This is one reason so many women enter into relationships with men who have no clue in this area—and reap the bitter consequences.

I cannot even imagine the solidarity of a relationship without the spiritual power that has guided my life and marriage. In my experience, most women are looking for a man who can both stimulate and steer them into a deeper understanding and relationship with God. Most women prefer a man who has a strong spiritual foundation and commitment to God. They feel that if he is spiritually mature and committed, then he also will be morally responsible in his relationship with her.

...many women find it a turn-on when a man is spiritually together and sincere about his relationship with God.

Women who are walking in a relationship with God themselves usually make this a priority, because they want to be certain that the man of their choosing has the ability to lead the family in prayer, Bible study, and church ministry involvement. This may sound surprising, but many women find it a turn-on when a man is spiritually together and sincere about his relationship with God. A woman who understands the plan and purpose of God when He created man and woman knows that her husband is the priestly leader in their home, and she depends on him to provide such a spiritual covering for their family. Most women who are spiritually mature will not in any way compromise in this area of their life.

I have learned from experience that the more I pray for my family, the stronger we become. As long as a man understands that he must stand daily as an intercessor for his wife and children, he will receive great respect and confidence from his wife. She knows that as long as he is praying, God will guide him. If he makes a mistake while doing so, she is confident that God will get him back on track, and she also will encourage him in this way.

A man will see what he is shown, but a woman will see what's actually there.

Spiritual security is a priceless commodity to a woman, and you can be certain that she knows when you are faking it, and when you are keeping it real. Let's not confuse church attendance with spiritual commitment. I know of men who will go to church on Sundays with the woman of their interest, just to make an impression. Women do not like a fake and pretentious man who talks one way and lives another. When it comes to spiritual matters, most women prefer to be in the same book as their mate, even if they are not on the same page, because at least she feels secure in knowing that ultimately he'll get there, and be stronger spiritually once he arrives.

FUTURE PLANNING

Planning for the future is another sensitive subject of concern for most women. Most women prefer to plan things well in advance because they do not like to be disappointed or discover that something they want to do does not work out. For example, a woman may go out to a special event on a Friday night, but you can be sure she began planning days ahead of time what she was going to wear.

Women are planners and thinkers, and they are analytical and detailed about everything that they do. Men look at the big picture, while women look at the whole picture. A man will see what he is shown, but a woman will see what's actually there. That is their nature, and as far as I can tell from my knowledge and experience with women, I don't think they are going to change.

If you plan to surprise a woman, be very selective and strategic in doing so, because women like to have their act together at all times. For example, if you are planning a surprise party for her that will have many people in attendance, find some way to make sure she looks her best. She won't appreciate being surprised by a large group of family and friends if her "face is a mess," or she is wearing "knockabout" clothes that do not present her to best advantage.

Women usually don't like surprise visits to their home unless they are given time to prepare the house for company. Men will invite people to the house even if it's not clean, but most women will not respond well to these kinds of incidents. Don't get me wrong; women love getting surprise gifts, but not surprise visits or anything that will catch them not at the top of their game. Women are planners and do not like to be caught off guard and forced to make decisions that do not afford her the opportunity of doing their due diligence.

For a woman, planning for the future is an important component of her relationship with a man that she either is seriously dating or already married to. This part of a woman's nature is often a deterrent to a man because he can easily misrepresent or misunderstand the motive behind her questions and concerns. For example, when a woman is dating a man and asks him questions about marriage, she is not trying to apply pressure to him. She's trying to understand the direction the relationship is going so that she does not allow her feelings to take her in a direction that will waste both time and emotions. It is the planning nature of the woman that causes her to respond in this way. Women need to know what time it is, so we men might as well adjust to it and flow with it.

When it comes to her future, a woman needs to know without question that her husband has every detail worked out in case something unforeseen happens. Men ought not be intimidated when their wives want to discuss things like vacations, children's college education, life insurance, and retirement. A woman concerned with things that relate to her husband's death does not mean she is planning for your death; it just means she is just trying to secure her future and the future of her children in case of an untimely or unexpected death.

Remember, women are planners; they have to know what they are going to do in situations that will require the support or resources of someone other than themselves. Most women like to do things themselves because they trust themselves more than they do others. Unfortunately, due to the decline of male responsibility within the world today, women have been forced to educate themselves and develop within their character a system of independence that affords them the level of security that they need. Women who depend totally on their men often find themselves drowning in the pool of low self-worth and purpose. They often feel as if they have no control over their destiny and their independence as women. This is why it is so important in marriage that the husband make sure that his wife doesn't feel as though she is being controlled by him simply because he is the sole provider.

I often tell husbands that it is a noble thing when we can make the kind of provisions for our families so that a second income is not needed. But that's no reason to pat ourselves on the back; we are only doing what we are supposed to do. It is important also for us to involve our wives in the decision-making process so that they feel they are contributing partners and not controlled persons. We should take the time together with them to discuss in detail everything about the future direction of the relationship. Do this, and I guarantee you that our wives will be much happier and much easier to live with.

SEX AND THE WOMAN

Tradition says that men love sex and women love security. This is a true statement, based upon the priority of need, but don't think for a minute that women don't love sex, because that would be a distortion of the truth. However, it is important to understand that women are very particular in the area of sex, and that for women, unlike men, sex does not start in the physical realm; it ends in the physical realm. For a woman, sex starts in the psychological realm and then moves outward from there. A man must learn to make love to his wife's mind before he can ever make love to her body.

A woman will never let her body take her where her mind hasn't gone first. She must feel her man before she will allow him to fill her. When a woman thinks of sex, she thinks of intimacy, which involves communication, caressing, and compassion, not just penetration. Women respond to sex so much better when their men take the sensitive approach. However, there are times when women like their men to be aggressive; it all depends on the moment. A woman needs to know that her man understands and knows the functionality of her body and her sexual desires. Nothing can be so annoying to a woman as to discover that her man doesn't have a clue as to what it takes to fulfill her sexual needs. Men can't think like men when it comes to sex with their wives; they must educate themselves as to the difference between male and female needs and drives.

Timing is another factor to consider when it comes to sex and women. Don't expect your woman to be intimate with you when there is tension and disagreement between you. A man can have sex with his wife and find release even if she is mad at him and not speaking, but she cannot. Even if she does, it will be out of her sense of duty, but it will leave her feeling used and humiliated.

There are times when a woman just doesn't want to have sex, and it has nothing to do with her feelings towards her husband. Women are thinkers and use their brains more than most men do. If she has things on her mind or is facing some emotional challenges that day, don't invade her space by attempting to engage her in sex. Try instead to listen to her, allowing her to unload her mind and settle her emotions. She will respect you all the more for that, and when she is ready, she will put something on you that you will never forget. That's just the way women are, and as men we have to love them for their creative natures and support their being different from us.

To avoid being disappointed or feeling rejected by your wife sexually, never assume that she is always ready to engage in sex activity with you. Conversation is a good way to find out where her mind is. Flirt with her just a little, stroke her gently, scope her out before you "go for the kill." If she flirts back, go to the next step; if she doesn't, back off and wait to see her reaction. Learn not to be pushy, but patient and observant. Find out what's on her mind, and make easing her mind your target, rather than sex. Remember, it's OK to wait; she'll still be your wife two hours later, or tomorrow.

Spontaneity is exciting and invigorating, but understanding is so much better.

It won't work if you make your woman feel that you are merely sex driven; she needs to know that you are into her as a total person. This is another form of the security she needs. Trust me, you will not die from lack of sexual fulfillment; find other ways of enjoying your wife while you wait on her to respond. Besides, it is so much better to have all of her when you are making love to her than just to have her body, because women know how to fake it, and that would not be good for your ego.

Sex between a husband and wife can be a beautiful and enjoyable adventure, but the two must have a communicable agreement in this area. Just as you plan everything else in your marriage, you have to plan your sexual relationship. Spontaneity is exciting and invigorating, but understanding is so much better. This will help to secure the relationship against any forms of rejection or disappointments that could cause devastating damage.

CHAPTER SEVEN

The Broken Rib

———◦◦◦———

"I never thought it could happen to us." Does that sound familiar? Many people live in denial as far as their marriages and relationships are concerned. They act as though they are exempt from the possibility of a troubled relationship, all the while ignoring the evidence around them that things are falling apart.

From the outset of this chapter I want to stress that no marriage, friendship, family or any other kind of a relationship is exempt from trouble. Some situations may be more severe than others, but no one will ever escape the net of negative situations that will grab them and pull them into its environment. So often we prepare ourselves only to handle the good times in our lives, but never educate ourselves about what to do when we face a crisis, or when we make a mistake and mess up on our mate.

The faith people tell us that if we anticipate trouble, we will expect it. I'm not suggesting that couples sit around anxiously anticipating trouble, but I am saying that they should talk about potential problems and develop a plan of action in advance, so that when something does happen, they can deal with it without it destroying their relationship.

One of the things I have learned about living in Florida, and especially south Florida, is that hurricanes are definite possibilities every year. After going through Hurricane Andrew in 1992, and having been in Miami for only two years, I learned that the key to surviving one of those horrifying storms is preparation. You cannot wait to prepare until a storm is on its way; you must make preparations before hurricane season even begins. This doesn't mean you are anticipating a hurricane—no one in his right mind wants to go through one of those—but simply that you are doing some advance planning, just in case.

...you have to be prepared for the unexpected.

It is the same way with a relationship; you have to be prepared for the unexpected. A careful and well thought out plan of action can help you recover in the event a life storm of disastrous proportions hits your home. Because we are not perfect people and do not live in a perfect world, we have to be ever conscious of those things that could make us vulnerable to such troubles. We must guard ourselves against the enemies that would lay traps to destroy our relationships.

Many voices of influence are always around us, vying for our attention and seeking to guide us. We must be very careful in discerning whose voices they are, where they come from, and whether or not they can be trusted. If you believe in the Word of God and are committed to that Word, then you should follow the principles contained within it and try those voices by the Spirit of God before you allow them to influence you. If you are not a believer, then you should at the very least seek counsel from positive people whom you trust to tell you the right thing to do.

The challenge we each face in our relationships is universal to man and has been since almost the very beginning. Genesis 3:1-6 reveals how the woman who was made from a rib of the man to be his helper was deceived by shrewd and influencing words of the serpent in the garden. Negative influences never appear in negative form, but they always have a negative agenda that will lead to a negative outcome. Eve listened to a subtle, deceptive and unfamiliar voice when she should have been listening only to the voices of her husband and of God. This placed her in a very vulnerable situation that she was unable to handle correctly, therefore leading to a break in the relationship between God and man.

Adam could have corrected the situation by simply not eating the fruit his wife offered him, but instead, he ate what she gave him. The resulting disaster not only affected them negatively, but required that God's whole plan for man be altered. This is why covering, preparation, and protection at all points are essential for the protection of our relationships. If we do not protect them, we open the door to failures that could destroy generations to come.

Ribs get broken when they are unprotected.

Ribs get broken when they are unprotected. I never thought that anyone would manipulate me and steal millions of dollars from me, but my naïveté numbed me from being realistic and guarded, enabling shrewd and unethical people to take advantage of me. It did not matter that I was a nice guy who would never hurt anyone on purpose. I allowed myself to be blinded by my own niceness and it almost cost me everything that I had and loved.

Never become so self-regarded that you lose sight of others and the world around you. Attentiveness is a critical factor in protecting any relationship. The moment you stop paying attention is the moment the relationship starts to drift off course and head for the rocks of conflict and destruction.

In this chapter we will consider several scenarios that could cause a relationship to become vulnerable. By vulnerable I mean unprotected and uncovered. These scenarios fall generally into two categories: taking each other for granted, and failing to communicate. Both are death to a relationship.

IGNORING THE SMALL THINGS

Here is a wisdom quote that expresses in a nutshell the danger of ignoring the small things in a relationship: *"Small things can become tall things that ulti-*

mately overshadow all things." When we ignore the little things in our relationships, we allow them to grow into major obstacles that block our partner's vision, preventing him or her from seeing that things are not as bad as they appear. After all, it is hard to see the pleasant, grassy, green valley when a barren, rocky mountain is in the way.

> *Do not discount the value of your partner's perspective simply because it is different from yours.*

People can only see what they see. An issue that may seem small to one person may be tall to another, and difficult to deal with. Do not discount the value of your partner's perspective simply because it is different from yours. Always give consideration to your partner's opinion, especially on a matter that affects both of you. Any affected party should have the opportunity to give input into the situation as well as maintain their freedom to act.

None of us has the right to force anyone to move from one place in life to another without his or her consent. The criminal justice system calls this kidnapping, and it carries a very high penalty. Relational kidnapping is a form of emotional bondage that many people endure on a daily basis. Issues of concern to them, even though they may be small, are routinely ignored by their partners, forcing them, for the sake of the relationship, to be silent and avoid making waves that could lead to a lot of conflict and debate within the home. Consequently, they die a little more each day, and so does the relationship.

What are these small things? They will vary from relationship to relationship because every person is different. To aid in understanding, however, I will allow you to take a sneak peek into my own personal relationship to get a snapshot view that might strike a responsive chord within your own heart.

All my life I have been a very ambitious and aggressive person when it comes to things I believe in and feel strongly purposed for. Fear of how something will turn out is never a consideration when I undertake a project.

I have the tendency repeatedly to allow whatever I am doing, whether led by divine inspiration or by personal aspiration, to take over all of my senses and sensibility. It has taken the writing of this book to awaken me thoroughly to the reality of my own ways.

Pamela, my wife of 27 years, operates from an entirely different frame of perspective and mental influence than mine. She is very guarded and careful when it comes to things such as we are discussing here. Pamela would rather we sit down and talk these things through to see if they are things we should consider doing at the time. The problem that causes me to resist her and ignore her concerns stems from the manner in which she presents them to me. From my perspective, her presentation can only damage or challenge my ego, but not the thing that I feel led to do. So I simply ignore her, because to me it is a small matter of fear and control on her part, so small that it does not warrant my attention or consideration.

Here's the problem. After so many years of this, Pamela became internally frustrated because my actions were causing her to feel insignificant in my life and in our marriage. The worst thing for a man to have on his hands is a frustrated female trying to fit herself into his very crowded life when he is not giving her any space. Such a state of affairs completely disrupts any sense of peace or comfort within the relationship. Sometimes Pamela's concerns may seem small to me, but I have learned the hard way that I could have prevented many costly mistakes and avoided a lot of friction in our relationship simply by listening to her and taking her concerns seriously. It took me a while to learn that what is small to me is not necessarily small to her. I learned the lesson, but I could have paid a cheaper tuition cost.

Strength and sense must not compete with each other, but complement each other and connect together. Strength says to a weightlifter, "Get down on that bench and lift three hundred pounds ten times." Sense says, "All right, but let me get me a spotter to help me so that these weights do not accidentally fall on me and crush my chest or break my neck."

I am not suggesting that men are the only ones who ignore the small things. Everyone is guilty. This problem is not gender-specific. All of us would do well to pay heed to the expressed concerns of our relationship partners, even if those concerns seem minor to us. They are not minor to our partners; otherwise, they would never have come up.

Take a few moments to evaluate yourself in this area. Are you guilty of ignoring or dismissing your partner's concerns as "small matters," allowing them to create a giant conflict in your relationship? Life is such a precious commodity, and having a healthy and peaceful relationship should be everybody's goal and desire. When you ignore the small things, you take it for granted that your partner is going to sit forever in silence without ever saying anything. That's a dangerous assumption, because you are fueling a fire that ultimately will lead to relationship burnout.

Don't let a mole hill turn into a mountain. Get a grip on those little things. Pay close attention to your mate, even to the little details; you will spare yourself a lot of unnecessary anguish. Let me share with you now a poem I wrote while working on this topic:

SMALL THINGS MATTER

It may be small but it is important you see

That you stop sometimes and listen to me.

Now I'm not trying to stop you from moving ahead,

I just want to know where I am being led.

I know how to follow without saying a word,

But just because I am quiet doesn't mean I should never be heard.

Small details can help you and save you some time,

If you put ten small pennies together, they'll give you a dime.

So don't just let our relationship dwindle away

Because you think you are the only person that should have something to say.

So let's learn to talk and respect each other's view,

I'll respect yours, no matter how small, and you respect mine too.

FORGETTING TO REMEMBER

One of the things that most people in a relationship have in common is the need to feel that their partner is conscious of their existence. All of us need the assurance that we matter to the person that we are committed to; that we are worth being remembered. No one wants to be an afterthought in the mind of his or her mate. Knowing that your mate has you locked firmly in his or her thoughts and consideration, and is aware of the things that are important to you, is a great comfort.

I want to challenge you to make it your business to remember important events and dates that affect your relationship. Many people, and men especially, tend to forget things like birthdays and anniversaries. Women, on the other hand, sometimes forget to say thank you or express their appreciation to their men. This is because women sometimes overplay the strength of a man and forget that men like the mushy stuff too. Men tend to allow their work and recreation to prioritize their agendas, and therefore often do not give their minds over to remembering details.

FORGETTING TO SAY "THANK YOU"

Let's consider a few things that can help us learn to stay focused on our mate and remember the important things. One of these is the simple step of saying thank you. Failing to express thanks when your mate does something for you is very inconsiderate, especially if it was something significant, or your mate made a special effort to be responsive to you. The size or significance of the act is irrelevant. No matter how big or small the deed may be, saying thank you is always appropriate.

Sometimes it is good to say thank you not for a gift given or a deed done, but simply out of appreciation for this person and for the privilege of having him or her in your life. Having someone to love you and be there for you is a very precious thing, and being careful and conscientious to say thank you helps that person feel appreciated and valued.

An attitude of gratitude determines the altitude by which we can excel into greater things in life.

As we have seen, it is often the small things ignored that cause hurt and create problems within a relationship. If your mate supports the things you do in your life without giving you grief, a thank you should always be on your agenda. My mother taught me that people do not have to be nice, and when they do, they do not have to choose you to be nice to, so always be grateful. When we say thank you to those we love, we affirm them in their significance as persons and as an important part of our lives.

Saying thank you doesn't take a lot of effort, just a little consideration. An attitude of gratitude determines the altitude by which we can excel into greater things in life. Saying thank you to your mate, or even a friend, is a positive virtue to which every decent person should aspire. "Thank you" says, "I value you and the effort that you put into doing what you do for me." It is a way of giving back to the person who gave to you. Saying thank you costs nothing, but yields great returns.

FORGETTING TO SAY "I LOVE YOU"

Some people seem not to have the need to hear the words, "I love you," from their partner, but I suspect they are not being honest. On the other hand, there are others who live to hear those three little (but giant) words from the lips of their mate. Generally speaking, men and women differ on this because of who they are by nature. Women seem to thrive more on hearing their man say, "I love you," and on him showing it by spending time with them and buying them nice and significant gifts. The gifts do not have to be expensive, but they do have to be well thought out.

For instance, fellows, if you buy your girl a card, make sure you do more than just look at the appearance of the card; read it carefully to ensure that it relates to you and the woman to whom you will be giving it. Rest assured, brothers, she will read it in detail, even if you don't, because she needs to know that you took the time to pick out the right card. She loves imagining you in the card aisle for minutes on end, reading through many cards until you found the one that was perfect for her. She expects you to do this, because that is exactly what she is going to do as it relates to you. This is a way that she hears and feels your love for her speak loud and clear.

Men hear love through sex and respect from their women. However, most men also love to hear their woman say, "I love you." Because everyone is different, it is important that you know your mate and what things he or she prefers. It's amazing how many married people have no clue as to their spouse's needs and preferences, even after many years of marriage. This ignorance is one of the critical

Know your mate, so that you can know how to fulfill his or her needs.

factors in the deaths of many marriages. Know your mate, so that you can know how to fulfill his or her needs. This is another way of saying, "I love you."

Saying "I love you" should be a daily practice because you never know when might be your last opportunity to say it to the one you love. Love expressed has tremendous power that can give strength and encouragement to your mate on a daily basis. Saying the words is, of course, only half of it; you also have to show your love and allow it to be the seasoning that brings flavor to your relationship. Love should be the influence by which we are governed and guided. True love has the power to cover all flaws, correct all failures, and complete all feelings. It is the common denominator within a relationship that gives balance to the relationship.

When you say, "I love you," to your mate, you are saying, "You are 'it' for me. I live to love you and am committed to that love."

When you do not make a practice of speaking your love daily, the opposite will occur and the effects could be devastating. All serious and healthy relationships are built on love. If at any time love becomes questionable, the whole relationship becomes questionable. This leads to insecurities on the part of the person who needs the constant affirmation. Do not dismiss as a small thing something that is important to your mate. Tell your mate, "I love you," as often as he or she needs to hear it.

I am not suggesting that speaking these three words should be some kind of daily duty or chore, but something motivated by your own choice and desire. If saying, "I love you" is a problem for you, it may be due to the fact that you really have no love for that person, and that *is* a problem. You cannot manufacture love; you cannot force yourself to love another person, neither can you force another person to love you. Love is a *choice*. It is part of your desired will and connection to another person. Any relationship should be ruled by truth and honesty, and being honest about love is the most important of all. Otherwise, you end up living a lie. Don't play around with the sensitive, fragile heart of another person. If you truly love that person, then make it your desired will and intent to tell him or her as frequently as possible.

COMPLAINING AND NOT COMPLIMENTING

One major cause of conflict, grief, and pain in relationships is when one partner hears almost nothing but complaints from the other, and rarely receives a compliment. People who complain all the time suffer from a lack of knowledge and are shortsighted with regard to the world that they live in. Complaining people are very difficult to live with because they have the tendency to wear out the nerves and patience of good and positive people. A chronic complainer can darken the day of even the sunniest and most optimistic person.

Complainers often are very heavy people emotionally, who bring unnecessary stress into situations because they lack the ability and or the desire to see life through a clear and clean window. Always clouded and controversial in every situation, they seek to control and seemingly lack the ability to appreciate what they have. From their point of view, everything is an issue that must be addressed immediately. They are extremely impatient people who want what they want, when they want it, the way they want it, every time they want it. Complainers often are reactors rather than responders; they speak before they think, careless of how their words or attitude may affect the other person.

It is impossible to please a complainer, because no matter what you do, it will never be enough. Their negative mindset makes them unable to recognize or acknowledge blessings in their life. Except for the fact that they are always negative, complainers are unpredictable; their reaction varies from situation to situation with no discernible pattern. Complainers are usually argumentative and fussy by nature, thriving on debate from a psychotic need to always be right in every situation. Trust comes hard for complainers and they usually are not good at keeping or managing relationships, which simply adds to the negativity in their lives. They constantly drive good people away from them, because good people who have a positive outlook on life find it very burdensome to remain in an environment of constant negativity and conflict.

As far as complainers are concerned, their complaints are always valid. It never seems to occur to them that perhaps the only legitimate complaint is the complaint itself, not the situation. There are times when complainers do have legitimate concerns, but they tend to shoot themselves in the foot with their overbearing and belligerent manner, causing others to become resentful and unwilling to assist them. Because they are not very affectionate people, complainers do not understand the relational value and importance of being sensitive instead of stern, patient instead of presumptuous, considerate instead of condemning, and grateful instead of grumpy.

Can you imagine having to live with such a person? Well, many people do, every day. Many people feel are so emotionally invested in their relationships—even negative ones—that the very possibility of some kind of a positive adjustment seems out of the question. It truly is amazing how opposites attract, which can be a good thing as long as the opposite attraction is a complement and not a conflict. It is never healthy to be in a relationship with someone who wants to fight over everything.

A healthy relationship is not always a stress-free relationship, because there will be times when challenges come. These challenges can either break a relationship or become opportunities and instruments for growth. Even when a relationship is not stress free it should be strife free. Excessive contention and strife can lead to resentment and ultimate chaos in a relationship, causing great division, and even the dissolution of the relationship. No one should ever have to continue in such a situation.

But how do you avoid it? First, be cautious about the people you get close to or allow to get close to you. Don't be overly anxious to jump into marriage or any other deep or emotionally invested relationships. It is important to know a person well before entering into a covenant relationship. Otherwise, you may discover too late that your dream mate is really a nightmare.

Constant complaining and negativity can kill a relationship, but a complimentary environment will build and strengthen it. Developing the practice of complimenting your mate, and other people in general, will produce very fruitful results. When you pay someone a compliment, you affirm and edify their self-esteem and value in ways that you could never imagine. A sincere compliment tells a person that you notice and appreciate the effort he or she has put forth to look good or do a good job.

In any relationship between two persons, whether married, engaged, dating, or just friends, complimenting is a strong method of building confidence, affection, and trust between them. Trust and confidence are key building blocks of any good and healthy relationship. The primary objective of doing something for someone you are in a relationship with is not necessarily for him or her to reciprocate as much as to appreciate. Appreciation shown is appreciation sown, and brings back a harvest of many more acts of kindness for the person who appreciates.

Paying compliments frequently is a habit that is easier to develop for some than for others. If you are one of those for whom this is a struggle, be encouraged in the knowledge that developing the habit of complimenting will be well worth every bit of time and energy you invest. However, it will require a true test of self and inner evaluation.

Appreciation shown is appreciation sown

There is no room for denial within yourself if you are going to accomplish the art of becoming complimentary. You may have to face some hard things about your personality that may be uncomfortable for you, such as selfishness, self-centeredness, and a tendency to be insensitive, inconsiderate, ungrateful, and controlling. Once you discover the joy of complimenting someone—not just their joy at receiving the compliment, but also your joy in giving it—you will never want to go back to being your old complaining self.

Spouses should be so in tune with each another as to notice immediately when one or the other sports a new look, adopts a new positive behavior, makes an honest effort to change an annoying behavior, or achieves a notable accomplishment—and be quick with a compliment. Such sensitivity will go far in building strength, peace, harmony and happiness in the marriage.

All of us like to be complimented every now and then, and more now than then. Even complainers like to receive compliments; they're just not very good at giving them. Compliment them often enough, however, and they may learn how.

Here is a poem that sums up what we have been discussing:

COMPLAINERS

Complainers are people who usually don't care,

They just go through life totally unaware.

They fuss and they argue and often complain,

About every little thing no matter how mundane.

They forget what they do have and focus on what they don't;

A word of appreciation they won't give, oh no, they just won't.

Complainers are short-sighted in their opinions and views,

They can wear out your nerves like an old pair of shoes.

No matter what you buy them, or how much you've spent,

It will snow in Miami before they pay you a compliment.

So if you are in search for a life-long mate, and you are romancing a complainer,

I would advise you to WAIT!

TOO LOUD TO LISTEN

"If you would stop talking so much and so loudly, you could hear what I am saying to you!"

How many times have you heard that statement? Or should I ask how many times you have made that statement to your partner? One of the most malignant killers of good relationships is when partners decide to tune each other out by ignoring each other's concerns, or drowning each other out by talking over each other. The ability and willingness to listen to each other is vital to the life and health of a relationship.

No one person in a relationship knows everything. Good communication, therefore, is crucial for the survival of a relationship. We've already talked about this in previous chapters. When partners can talk about anything and everything without either one feeling left out of the conversation, it is a sign of a healthy and growing relationship.

Why do some people in a relationship become too loud to listen? What's all that noise about anyway? Let's see if we can unwrap some of the psychology behind the loud fussing and rage that is sometimes verbalized when people try to communicate. Personality deficiencies of one kind or another often lie at the heart of certain individuals' tendency to fly off the handle during a family "discussion." Are these individuals trying to make a point, or are they trying to avoid a point they don't want to hear, a point that would be made if the loud individual would simply quiet down? Hmm, sounds like a coverup to me.

1. The Scare Tactic. Loudness of speech is often a scare tactic employed to cover up a person's insecurity in the area of communication. Some people feel that if they get aggressively loud it will give them an edge over their partner in getting their point across. They assume that if they can talk over their partner, their partner will pay more attention to their point. In actuality, the opposite is more likely to occur, depending on the strength of the individual whom the loud person is trying to drown out.

Allow me to use myself as an example: if you scream at me, you automatically lose all my interest in listening to you. I would like to think that I am a reasonably intelligent person and can handle a sensible conversation. So when a person gets loud with me from the outset of the conversation, that person has already insulted me and caused me to assume a defensive position. Being on the defensive while talking with someone is not a comfortable form of communication, because you spend most of your time forming mental strategy for your next response, and therefore have no ear to listen to the other person's concerns.

People who use loudness of tone to be heard are often trying to magnify a point to add validity to its importance, especially a weak point. However, they have the tendency to make things bigger than they really are. A loud person's need to be seen and heard frequently stems from some sort of insecurity or frustration. This is why I encourage couples never to address an issue with their mates while angry and emotionally frustrated. Frustration is the fuel that will aggrandize an issue, causing a fire of emotionally heated fussing and argument, which could cause each person to say some things they do not mean. And words once spoken can never be recalled.

...words once spoken can never be recalled.

Words spoken in anger can be very damaging to a person's ego, self-esteem, and self-worth. Trying to retract negative comments you have made is like trying to draw back into your lungs the same air you have just breathed out; it can't be done. Once it's out, it's out. Now you have to deal with the damage you've caused to a person's emotional or mental stability. Get your anger and temper under control before you run good people out of your life forever. Learn how to communicate without shouting and fussing. Stop insisting that shouting is the only way anyone will hear what you are saying. Here is a wisdom quote: *"It is better to say nothing in silence than to say everything that you want to say by screaming."*

People who talk loudly often find it very hard to hear what the other person is saying. Tone it down and pay close attention to your partner; make sure that you do not dominate the conversation. If you are a person facing this challenge, ask your partner or friends to pull your coattail when you begin to get loud, and be willing to listen and respond when they do. You will not change overnight, especially if this has become a part of your personality. In fact, you may never be completely free from this behavior, but through matured moderation, you should be able to bring it under control. Think about how much more inviting it will be for your partner or friends to communicate their feelings and concerns to you when you stop all of your erratic behavior of loudness and fussing. Get it together, because if you don't, it could cost you more than you really want to pay.

Consider the words of this poem about listening:

LISTEN

Can I get a word in so that I can be heard in?

I'm tired of your fussing and screaming
and you not understanding what I'm meaning.

I'm trying to make a statement, I'm trying to make a point,
but your loud and crazy behavior is about to make me leave this joint.

You keep raising your voice, hey what's that all about?

Do you think that all of your noise will soon just drown me out?

Well, you'd better think about it, and you'd better think twice,
'cause when I do get a chance to speak, it's not going to be nice.

So stop talking so much and listen to me,
I need to have something to say, if the two of us are going to be.

Now that's so much better, since you've changed your tone,
I just wanted to tell you,

He who has not learned to listen, has not yet grown.

2. The Trust Factor of Communication. Effective communication in a relationship is birthed out of the womb of trust. No one will ever communicate his or her true feelings to someone else unless a high level of confidence and trust has been established between them. People simply will not confide in those whom they do not and cannot trust. Trust is a strong yet sensitive virtue: powerful for building lasting relationships, but easily injured. Once lost, trust can be very difficult to restore.

Honest and open communication in a relationship is a most precious, rewarding, and too often rare, commodity. If communication in a relationship is strained, so is trust, and if trust is strained, the relationship is under dangerous stress. Relationships are never completely free of problems or challenges, but when two people can talk them out, they can also work them out without any outside support or intrusion. We humans often seem to forget that we are subject to making repeated mistakes, but when we know that we have a friendship with another person and can confide in that person, it makes dealing with the situation so much easier.

I tell people all of the time that I am glad that the God of the Bible is so willing to listen to our issues, because even when He judges us, He does so with a hand of pure and sure unconditional love. Unfortunately, people are not like God; learning to trust another person can be a very fearful prospect, because trust can be easily betrayed. It is with that in mind that I want to share with you what I call, "The Four Fear Factors of Trust," four primary fears that prevent people from placing trust in another person:

a. Fear of being judged without a fair trial.

b. Fear of being misunderstood without being allowed to give some clarity to the issue at hand.

c. Fear of being rejected by those whom they need to feel that they are accepted by.

d. Fear of being uncertain about their ability to recover what they've lost.

The existence of any of these factors in a relationship can create brokenness that will not heal by itself. Ignoring the issue will only make matters worse. These are major issues that must be addressed, or else the relationship will be torn apart with no possibility of repair. No relationship is healthy as long as there exist little idiosyncratic importances that keep getting swept under the carpet of insensitivity, while being walked on by the feet of complacency and overrated confidence. One person may think that everything is all right, but if both parties are not saying the same thing, it is not all right, and the relationship is dying, slowly but surely.

Things get broken when they are mishandled or handled carelessly. Careful attention to detail must be given when it comes to relationships, especially marriage. Men, by nature, are not as detail-oriented as women; therefore, they must put forth the effort to become so for the sake of the women in their lives. It is also so important for the ladies to give some extra praise when their man gives attention to things that are important to them. Trust me; it takes a lot for a man to be very detailed when it comes to his woman.

Men should also understand the importance of giving time regularly to communicating with their woman on a routine basis so that she can share with him her concerns. This protects the relationship from the emotional explosions that would certainly occur if she did not have the opportunity to express herself in full detail.

Women must be allowed to talk; it's their nature that drives them to obtain knowledge. That's why most women today are more educated than men; they have this driving need within them for knowledge. This is not to say that all women are like this, there are a few who have such low self value that they become isolated within themselves for the purpose of self security.

Women must be allowed to talk; it's their nature that drives them to obtain knowledge.

For the most part, this has to do with their upbringing more than their nature. People who have been scared tend to stray away from the normalcy of their human personality. If you find a woman who does not like to communicate, you will find a woman who probably has a history of negative issues that have caused her to be silent. She wasn't born that way; she's been torn that way.

Wherever there is excessive fear, there is the possibility of failure or constant frustration. Fear is a source of insecurity that will take the fire out of anyone or anything that gives in to its controlling and destructive power. As far as a relationship is concerned, it is vitally important that couples work hard to help each other overcome any and all insecurities and fear through effective communication and support. Relationships are often destroyed when high levels of insecurities and fears exist. We discuss this in more detail in chapter nine.

A PRAYER FOR YOU

Dear Father, I bless You for Your unchangeable and unbreakable love that You give to all of us who will accept it. I pray, Father, for all of those who have and are experiencing brokenness within their relationships. Through Your Word, Your Spirit, and the principles laid out here, may you let them find the strength and comfort that will enable them to restore and repair their broken relationships. May they search You out with their hearts, You who are the God who is able to heal and fix any situation, and find Your healing hands to rest upon their situations. I thank You, Father, for Your willingness to comfort us and sustain us in and through these times. I bless You in advance for the many testimonies of healings and deliverances that will come as a result of Your ministry through this book. Thank You for Your forgiveness that You so graciously grant to those of us who stand in need of it daily. Father, please give Your watchful care over every marriage and over every single person, whomever he or she may be. I thank You for these things in the name of Jesus, Amen.

CHAPTER EIGHT

Stop the Wedding, The Marriage is in Trouble!

———⋅>•⋅<———

Excitement is in the air, laughter lingers in every setting, and the sounds of happiness are on the lips of everyone involved. Nervous tension and pre-panic attacks are common, due to the desire for everything to be perfect. Months of meetings between the responsible parties have discussed in detail and worked out all the particulars to ensure that this is a lifelong event. Family and friends are praying and making expensive purchases to add a touch of elegance that will have the tabloids and the gossip community gazing in envy and admiration.

Then there are the bridesmaids, the groomsmen, the maid of honor, the matron of honor, the best man, the flower girls, the ring bearer, the ushers, the photographer, the musicians, the limo, the caterer, the cake, the expenses, and the stress. The focus lies heavy on this one-day event that we call, "The Wedding."

How wonderful and spectacular these events have become in our society today. People compete with each other to see who can have the biggest and most elegant wedding. Even *The Today Show* has an annual competition to see who will be chosen as the couple to receive an all-expenses-paid wedding ceremony and honeymoon. A new reality show called *Bridezilla* depicts the often-negative stress and strain that people go through just to prepare for a wedding.

I am not a wedding hater. On the contrary, I think engaged couples should do whatever they can afford to do—or can afford to live with—to make their wedding day a never-to-be-forgotten occasion. My purpose in this chapter, however, is not to bring focus or attention to ceremonial fancy, but to unlock the door to real heart to heart conversation and study on the marriage itself. I am convinced that where marriage is concerned, we sometimes give too much attention to the things that do not have eternal essence or value and not enough to the most important things that will affect the lives of the couple: the relational, spiritual and eternal elements.

Too many people hurry into marriage with insufficient knowledge of the person to whom they are wed.

Outstanding issues that are not dealt with before the wedding could cause a relapse in the relationship, preventing it from being able to survive a crisis. When a marriage hits those uncomfortable bumps that are sure to come at some point, the partners need to have the security of endurance in order to move beyond the challenge.

One of the most devastating and difficult to survive elements in a relationship is the element of surprise. It is not a light matter, once you are married, for your spouse to reveal to you something about himself or herself that you neither knew nor had any suspicion about, especially when it is serious enough to have a bearing on your relationship. For example, the revelation of previously undisclosed sexual promiscuity or idiosyncratic behavior would create major problems for your marriage. At the very least, trust would be seriously damaged. Such a bombshell could easily tear the very fabric of a relationship into shreds with no hope of repair.

Too many people hurry into marriage with insufficient knowledge of the person to whom they are wed. They stand at the altar of some church or cathedral, or on some exotic island retreat site, and commit their lives to someone who is almost a complete stranger to them.

Try to imagine the situation. The wedding is done, all the fanfare is over, the honeymoon is past and all the wedding gifts have been acknowledged with thank you notes. The heady excitement of those early days has faded and a more mundane reality has set in. The two of you are sitting there together one day when all of sudden, out of the mouth of your spouse come thoughts and philosophies that totally contradict your belief system. You are shocked, because you had no idea your spouse felt or believed this way about those issues. Now you find yourself having to have discussions about basic philosophies and fundamental beliefs and values that you should have addressed before either of you said, "I do."

It is probably impossible to anticipate beforehand every issue that might come up during a couple's married life, but they should take the time to get to know each other well and to explore thoroughly the most basic and important elements and issues such as faith, finances, parenting philosophies and desires, personal dreams, goals, and ambitions, moral and ethical standards, and past sexual history (if any). Many marriages are doomed from the beginning because the partners did not take the time to talk and truly get to know each other, or to undergo careful and competent counseling before entering into a covenant agreement with each other. When a couple places more emphasis on preparing for the wedding than on preparing for the marriage, the consequences can be devastating.

In this chapter we will examine some of the tender topics that couples often neglect until it is too late.

WE NEED TO DEAL WITH THIS

Unresolved issues comprise one of the most common areas of conflict that couples bring with them into a marriage relationship. Many couples end up frustrated in their marriages because they made the mistake of sacrificing truth for feelings. No relationship is healthy as long as there are unpleasant truths about each other that a couple may have discussed but never dealt with.

This brings into play what I have labeled as the "NOP syndrome," which stands for, *Neglected On Purpose*. This is the syndrome in which, out of a desire to avoid conflict, you deliberately overlook a negative trait, behavior, belief, value, or other issue in your prospective mate that is in direct conflict with your own. Just because you act as though you don't see that speeding train coming down the track toward you doesn't change the fact that it is really coming. You try crossing the track anyway, and, *"Bam!"* you just got slammed without the possibility of recovery. Because you became so emotionally attached to this person, and because the relationship was moving towards marriage, you swept those issues under the rug of a false expectation that they would go away, only to discover that they did not.

Any issues within a relationship that could cause damage to the relationship, if not dealt with, ultimately will reappear at some point with even greater damage potential. Neglecting an issue does not make it go away, except, perhaps, in your own mind. Don't be so desperate to get married that you ignore those issues that need resolution before the wedding. If you are at odds with your prospective mate on certain issues before the wedding, and get married anyway, without resolving those issues, you are setting yourself up for a crippled and handicapped marriage. The only thing that can give life and sustenance to a relationship is truth and the resolution of all conflicting issues.

A very close friend of mine was on his way to a major investment meeting that was going to provide him with some very important information that would save him hundreds of thousands of dollars and make him millions of dollars. While on his way to the meeting, however, he drove through an area where the police were doing a random security check. They pulled him over and asked to see his driver's license. After running a check on his tag number, the officers asked him to step out of the car. They read him his rights and arrested him because there was an outstanding arrest warrant for him.

Here he was, all frustrated, not knowing what the problem was. He was taken to the local police station and booked for failure to pay some traffic tickets. These tickets were unpaid parking citations that he knew he had, but had neglected to pay them, as if he thought they would just go away. All he had needed to do was to pay the tickets, which totaled only two hundred dollars. Because he neglected to deal with these outstanding issues, he missed the investment meeting and lost a great deal of money. So much for the unimportance of unresolved issues!

How many marriages have this same problem, where people go into marriage knowing that there are things that need to be dealt with, and they just neglect them? They have these glamorous weddings and expensive honeymoons, only to discover that they are living a lie. Why does this happen?

Some people hide behind a false reality because they fear being alone. Others do it for the sake of their image or to make an impression on their family and friends. I see this so often that I want to scream out loud to couples, *"Deal with it!"* Stop avoiding issues of concern that you have with your mate. Ask all the questions you feel you need to ask, and don't commit to that person until you get answers that satisfy your questions and concerns. Place enough value on yourself and on the sanctity of marriage that you do not compromise the validity of your concerns and convictions. Remember, anything that you do not confront you will never conquer. Confronting an issue before you get married is so much better than running the risk of that thing becoming a sore source of conflict within your marriage.

Remember, anything that you do not confront you will never conquer.

It is so much better to know before the wedding that you are willing to live with the final conclusion concerning the issues of your mate. At least you have discussed them and put into place a plan of resolution to help the two of you deal with them. Conflict resolutions are strategies that can be employed to help your marriage when conflict occurs. I always urge couples to have these strategies in place before the wedding, instead of waiting until afterwards. Trust me when I tell you that it is much cheaper and more peaceful to handle these issues, whatever they are, before purchasing that gown and that ring and all of those other expensive things.

Be smart; be wise. Make the firm decision now that you will not live in a relationship where you and your partner do not deal with your issues. Why get married just for the sake of being married, and end up miserable? Pray to God to help you face the truth and live by it, no matter the outcome. Truth is so much easier to deal with beforehand than the tragedy of having to come out of a relationship because truth after the fact proved too damaging to handle. Don't lean with it, don't rock with it, just "deal with it."

YOU DIDN'T TELL ME THAT

Almost as bad as unresolved issues is the problem of *undisclosed information.* This issue develops when one person in a relationship makes the decision to withhold information about himself or herself from the other. Sometimes both persons play this game. It is vitally important that couples share information about themselves and their circumstances beforehand so there will be no little pop-ups down the road. Truthful information shared takes the power of blame or excuse out of the communication equation in a relationship. Once you have shared information with your mate concerning your likes, dislikes, preferences, and challenges, you prevent them from being able to say, "I didn't know that," because you have been open and honest with them from the beginning. They are then without excuse if these issues come up.

The whole purpose of reading and studying is to gain knowledge, and knowledge is acquired through the acquisition of information. It is impossible to be effective in any area of life without proper data or information. We need information in order to process our thoughts and opinions on any subject. As far as relationships are concerned, no one should expect to have a healthy and fruitful relationship when information about one or both of the subjects has been withheld. Your partner has a right to your information, especially if that information will affect them if they marry you. And you have a right to your partner's information. No wise person will become deeply involved in a relationship without asking all the important questions and waiting for all the right answers before making a commitment.

There are some secrets that can be devastating to a relationship if they are made known only after two people are married. We will discus several below. It should be easy to see why these particular issues will cause marital conflict if they are not disclosed beforehand.

I can't have children. I once counseled a couple that had this issue. The wife had been informed by her physician that she could not have children because of some abnormality with her uterus. But she never shared this information with her future mate, even after the relationship began to get serious, and even though she knew he loved children. He never asked about it, so she never said anything.

Stick to your principles without compromise.

When I asked her why she did not tell him, she responded that she had faith in God to heal her, so she did not bother to mention it. Being a man of faith, I knew I had to address her response very carefully. I told her that she did not have total faith in God, because if she really had faith in God, she would have told her mate and trusted God to not allow it to be a hindrance to their relationship.

Besides, although faith in God is critically important for any truly healthy relationship, faith in one's partner is also important. Sometimes we use spiritual reasoning without biblical responsibility or accuracy. If you are going to follow the spiritual path, don't compromise that path by detouring just because you come to a challenging stretch of the road. Stick to your principles without compromise.

There are many adoption alternatives available for childless couples, so if this is your problem, be honest and up front about it. Being open at the beginning is so credible in these situations. If your prospective mate is really in love with you and wants to spend his/her life with you, then not being able to have children will not destroy the relationship. And if it does, that person was not right for you anyway.

I'm bi-sexual. This has been a topic of much media attention in recent years due to the number of men revealing to their spouses that they were on the down low. You can call it "on the down low" if you want, but it is a very low down thing to purposely play with the emotions and esteem of another person by withholding such serious information. This is the highest possible form of manipulation and deception. It is also selfishness to the utmost degree, and deserves to be punished to the highest degree.

Seeking to control a person's life by withholding personal information about yourself that would enable that person to make an informed decision about your relationship, even choosing to take a different route, is self-seeking and completely immoral. Forcing your view on another against that person's will and desire is a form of psychological rape and abuse. No excuse can possibly justify behavior such as this, and the person is well within his or her rights to leave.

I have heard reasoning such as, "I thought that I was over that part of my life," and, "That was in my past," and, "I wasn't sure about my sexual preference; I just thought it was a phase that would pass." It doesn't matter if this is a part of your history or mystery, you owe it to the person who is in relationship with you to share this information so that he or she can receive proper counsel and make an informed and deliberate decision about what to do. Remember, the other person has freedom of choice that you should never take into your own hands. This relates not only to bi-sexual men, but also to bi-sexual women.

I have sexual insecurities. Believe it or not, sex is often a subject that is neglected within relationships that are moving towards marriage. As a Christian man of god, I believe strongly that sex between two persons should be pre-served for marriage. However, there are some realities that we simply must face. One of these is the fact that the majority of people who get married today, professing Christians included, are having sex with their partners before marriage.

The other reality that we must face is the one we are dealing with here. Even if you are not going to have sex with your mate until after marriage, that does not excuse you from conversation on the topic. If you know that you are a per-son with a lot of sexual insecurities, then you should be seeking some sound counsel in this area. I would even advise that both parties attend these sessions together so that they can both know what to expect and how to get through the process together.

We develop sexually in our minds and thoughts before we ever become involved sexually.

Here is a truth: most people know what their sexual tendency is even before they ever have sex. We develop sexually in our minds and thoughts before we ever become involved sexually. That's why some people can't wait to be married before they have sex, because they cannot resist the temptation of their creative sexual thoughts.

Some people are comfortable with the idea of sexual freedom and look forward to being able to share with their mate a life of sexual passion and intimate eroticism once they are married. Then there are those, on the other hand, both men and women, who have had a negative exposure to sex at an early age. Sexual abuse is a common cause behind many people becoming insecure or uncomfortable with being sexually free with their mate. People in this situation often choose not to disclose such information to their prospec-tive mate because they find it too painfully embarrassing or humiliating. Fear of rejection often plays a factor too. This is not good, because sex is a major part of a marriage, and two people who share the same marriage bed should share the same views on sex.

According to the Bible, sex consummates a marriage, not the wedding. If you are one of those who has suffered sexual abuse, you need to be open about this issue and discuss it with your partner *before* the wedding. If you put it off until after you are married, you will be setting up yourself and your spouse for a lot of heartache. I would go as far as to say that any person who has not overcome his or her childhood abuses is not ready to make a marriage commitment.

It is not good to begin a marriage with unsolved mysteries. Let your partner know just what your issues are, and just maybe the two of you together can work through them. If not, it is better to find that out now, before the marriage, than to discover later on that the two of you are not sexually compatible. Any hang-ups that either of you carry into your marriage will ultimately cause your marriage to get hung up, preventing it from being the beautiful blessing that God has ordained for it to be. Do not allow yourself to be hindered by your sexual misfortunes. Pray and ask God to help you to find healing in this area. Do not spend your life as a prisoner to the person who robbed you of your sexual innocence. Take your haunted and horrifying memories of pain and lay them at the feet of Christ. Assert your God-given authority over this thing, because if you do not, your marriage will never be healthy. Remember, God created sex for enjoyment between a man and a woman committed to each other in a covenant of marriage. Each should have the freedom to share his or her feelings and emotions without restrictions or reservations.

I have a life-threatening disease. This is a quite serious matter, especially if the disease is transferable, sexually or otherwise. In a world where HIV and AIDS are spreading at epidemic rates in some regions, and where many other physically damaging sexually transmitted diseases are on the rise, couples have to concern themselves with the health of the person that they are in relationship with.

Before walking that marriage aisle, make it your business to know about your partner's health. And if you really love and care about your partner, you will be open and up front about your own. It doesn't matter what it is—cancer, high blood pressure, diabetes—you need to be completely honest with each other. Both of you are entitled to know what you are getting with each other. Failing to inform your mate of your life-threatening illness would be a major form of deception.

I remember one situation where a woman knew of her friend's sickness, but was determined to live with him through it. She was even preparing to marry him, but he died before reached that point. The beautiful part of this story is that he told her of his condition in advance, giving her the option either to walk away or continue on. Because of her unconditional love for him, she stayed the course, and was right there by his side when he passed.

Certainly, none of us know what tomorrow holds. You could get married today and you or your mate could die tomorrow; that would be something beyond your control. But if you know you are dying, or face years of steadily degenerating health, you have a responsibility to let your partner know what he or she is getting into by starting up a relationship with you.

Not being open with your mate for any reason is a cop-out to avoid a possible drop out.

Not being open with your mate for any reason is a cop-out to avoid a possible drop out. Trust the truth; it will always provide you with a place of comfort and peace. If necessary, have your attending physician help you in this process by sitting down with your mate and explaining in detail everything there is to know about your condition. And here's another point: prescription medications frequently have certain side effects. Your mate needs to know what medications you are taking and what possible side effects to watch out for, so he or she can support you on the basis of knowledge rather than speculation.

DO I HAVE TO DO THAT?

Another common problem that crops up in marriage relationships is the problem that I call the **undesirable imaginative**. This is when one partner in a relationship tries to coax, cajole, pressure, or coerce the other into an action or position that goes far beyond that partner's passion, desire or will. In other words, this problem arises whenever you try to pressure your partner into doing something he or she does not want to do, or when your partner does the same to you. The scope of this problem is virtually unlimited, because it can relate to so many areas: money, sex, domestic responsibilities, religion, family relations, etc.

Marriage is serious business. Unlike dating, where if you don't like something, you either work it out or just walk away, marriage is a lifelong commitment; you can't just "walk away." Your responsibilities toward each other in marriage should never be seen merely as "duty," but should be done out of a genuine spirit of desire to satisfy each other. Whatever pleases your mate should become pleasure for you, because the realm of love in marriage is supposed to be ruled by a spirit of unselfishness. Love does not seek its own way, but focuses more on the other person. That is why couples should talk openly about all things before they get married, because one of the most powerful declarations that you make in marriage is the simple phrase, "I do."

Just because you do not desire something or feel comfortable about something doesn't necessarily mean your spouse does not, or even should not. Compatibility within a marriage is important for the survival and peace of that marriage. Married couples must learn to co-exist with each other. This will only happen when there is clarity of thought, mind, desire and will. You cannot have a healthy marriage based on speculation; in order for there to be harmony, you each have to know what is expected. There is no room for surprises after the wedding, because not everybody can handle surprises. When you say, "I do," you are saying, "I commit to the responsibility of fulfilling the needs of my mate."

So often couples make the mistake of committing before connecting. This puts them in a position where co-existing is almost impossible because of their inability to agree. Couples need to connect before they commit.

One of the many things I love about the Word of God (Holy Bible) is that it lays out before us the promises of God and the requirements necessary for us to enjoy those promises. My relationship with God is a personal and open relationship that does not allow room for any cover up.

Marriage should be the same way. The integrity of your relationship with the person you have chosen to marry rests solely upon your willingness to convey to each other all of your expectations without compromise. Do not waver in this area, because if you discover a need that your spouse has that you find undesirable or too much of a challenge to fulfill, you release upon your spouse a spirit of rejection that could lead to some very difficult times in your marriage. This is not an issue to take lightly, but it should be handled carefully and with sensitivity. You should not automatically assume the position of, "There's no way I am going to do that," but you should communicate your differences in the matter and strive to find a place of agreement between you and your mate.

Remember, peace between you and your mate should always be your goal. Flexibility and change are always necessary whenever you choose to enter into a relationship with someone. It is much better to have this conversation before you get married than to be forced by circumstances to have it after the wedding, when it may be too late. Being straight with your mate now will help to negate future misunderstandings regarding important issues and feelings.

I THOUGHT YOU WERE PAST THAT

Sometimes married couples, or couples preparing for marriage, get troubling issues out in the open, work through them, and think they have put those issues behind them, only to have them pop up again some time down the line. This is the problem that I call, *undefeated idiosyncrasies*. Here's a scenario: It is six months after the wedding and your marriage just hit a big bump because your mate is not responding to you in a certain area. You do not understand what the problem is, because the two of you discussed this issue and your mate led you to believe it was resolved. Yet, here it is again.

Undefeated idiosyncrasies are those certain characteristic emotional and mental challenges, issues, and hang-ups that people struggle with and pretend to be over, but in reality have never conquered. All of us have some little "demons" in our personality and makeup that we strive daily to overcome, but that is not the issue. The issue is the return of a problem or hang-up that both of you had concluded would no longer be an issue in your marriage. This reveals either one of two things: one of you was lying when you said the issue was resolved, or you honestly thought you were over it but discovered that you are not. Now you both have to do some serious marital damage control in order to save your relationship.

The truth of the matter is that it is going to take a joint effort in order for this to be resolved and the restoration of trust secured. You cannot do this on your own; you need your mate's support and complete understanding. The stronger person has to assume the major role in this scenario, while the weaker partner must feel that support without compromise. If you truly love each other and are committed to the marriage, then pride and broken promises must cease to be the controlling factors in the mind of the wronged person. Being wronged by your mate does not release you from the responsibility of helping him or her with the reparation stages that will be required to fix the damage. Marriage is a for-better-or-for-worse proposition, and you must find the needed supports in order to move beyond the challenge. The marriage is never over until one of you says it is over, so work at it with much diligence and openness.

Once again I want to stress that these are things that could be avoided if couples would give more attention to the marriage and less attention to the wedding. I know that many people have these fairy-tale weddings in their minds, but what sense or cents does it make to have an illustrious wedding and an illusion of a marriage. Give attentive detail to your mate and make sure that you are in agreement on all major matters, because, even though the wedding lasts only a few hours, your marriage lasts a lifetime. What's worth the most investment, the wedding or the marriage? If you do not agree that it is the marriage, then you need to just throw yourself a big party and call it a day.

> *What's worth the most investment, the wedding or the marriage?*

Here is a poem that summarizes this chapter and unveils the place where many relationships find themselves—the place of illusion:

ILLUSIONS

I wish we had known how different we were,

Then you could have had another him, and I could've had another her.

So here we are, so indecisive after only a few years,

And our marriage has been reduced to just memories and tears.

I just didn't know and I didn't bother to ask,

And now you're asking me to do some things and I'm not up to the task.

So I guess we're married strangers who don't have a clue,

Because you say you don't know me, and I know I don't know you.

The times that we talk are nothing but conversation,

But our talk is so bland because we have no relation.

Did we spend most of our time not paying attention?

Or did we really see it coming, but were consumed by pretension?

So what do you do when you end up in such a crazy place?

Is there a solution to the confusion that we both must now face?

It's amazing how reality sets in after the fact,

And you find that your wedding was only an expensive act.

But now that the wedding is over and all of the guests are gone,

You've got pictures and presents, but you are feeling so alone.

Well, it is what it is without questions or doubt,

So do we just walk away, or do we try to work it out?

Well that's a decision that each individual will have to decide,

But if you choose to work it out, you must stand by each other's side.

So I guess if you don't ask questions of the person you say is for you,

Then you might as well stop the wedding before you say, "I Do."

CHAPTER NINE

Spare Ribs

———————

Spare ribs? What a strange topic for a book on marriage and relationships! Sounds more like something you would expect to see in a cookbook or on the menu at the local barbecue establishment!

Seriously, in this concluding chapter I will be talking not about food but about marital infidelity. The phrase "spare ribs," as used in this chapter, refers to the non-spousal person with whom a dissatisfied and unfulfilled married person seeks to find the comfort, compassion, companionship, commonality, and sexual release that are missing in his or her marriage. In other words, this chapter is about the "other woman," the "other man," and what marriage partners can do about the problem to save and renew their marriage.

Before we begin, I want to make my own position on infidelity very clear: *There is never any excuse for a married person to have a spare rib.* God's design for marriage is one man and one woman for life. There are, however, many "reasons" that our secular society offers to explain or justify why marriage partners so often choose to be unfaithful to each other.

God's design for marriage is one man and one woman for life.

We live in a world that largely denies the fundamental sinfulness of human nature. This leads, on the one hand, to the tendency to excuse marital infidelity and other moral "failures" as the natural outworkings of an evolved species, and on the other, to become insensitive and overly judgmental of human frailty. This is why God, the Creator of humanity, seeks to transform the mind and heart of man, because apart from a spiritual transformation, man will continue to make decisions that are in direct conflict with the truth and order that God established and holds him accountable to.

My position is never to be judge or jury, but an intercessor who stands in the gap, praying and encouraging people to walk in a way that would please God. In today's society, married couples must undertake a united, conscious moral stand to preserve the sanctity of their marriage and to keep it pure and infidelity-free. In order to succeed, both partners must want it passionately, work at it deliberately and walk faithfully through all the necessary processes to achieve it. Don't be so naïve as to say, "It could never happen to us." Many of the people I have counseled who had to face the devastating pain of infidelity have admitted to me that they never saw it coming. It hit them all of a sudden. So don't assume it will never happen to you.

One of the problems that we face is that often there is not enough pre-counsel given to couples to help them avoid this infrequently talked about occurrence. Consequently, many new marriages soon join the ranks of those relationships in which one or both partners, for whatever reason, are involved in secret affairs outside their marriages. It is because of this frequent lack of counsel and knowledge that I want to speak very candidly and openly on this subject with the prayer that couples whose marriages have been wracked by the storm of infidelity will find hope, healing, and restoration of their relationships. My prayer also is that those couples that have not yet had to deal with infidelity will gain the knowledge, wisdom and insight to ensure between themselves that it never happens.

Infidelity infects every segment of society. No amount of education, financial status, social status, or even religious faith makes any of us automatically immune. Infidelity can strike anytime, anywhere. But forewarned is forearmed. In this chapter I will share some common factors that can make a marriage vulnerable to this devastating relationship killer. I sometimes call "spare ribs" the "comfortable danger" because they are relationships that are easy to get into but hard to get out of without causing many casualties. Any time a married person gets emotionally or sexually involved with someone other than his or her spouse, somebody's going to get hurt.

Unfortunately, some marriages never recover from the devastation of infidelity. Couples at the marriage altar easily speak the words, "for better or worse, until death do us part," and they usually mean it—until a challenge comes along that requires them to uphold that declaration. I always say that it is easy to say what you will do when no one is asking you to do it.

To most people, the word "commitment" is conditional, but in truth it is unconditional in both its etymological and creative sense. Never declare what you will or will not do until you have had the challenge or opportunity to do it, and are able to walk away with the integrity of your word still in place. Even then, you have not earned "bragging rights," because all the good that any of us are able to do is prompted and provided by the divine empowerment that we get from God, who alone is perfect and good. Here is a wisdom tip: *"Stop bragging; you haven't left earth yet."*

As we prepare to enter into an unveiling of truth without theoretical conjecture or philosophical persuasive reasoning, I challenge you in advance to remove anything from your mind that would prevent you from remaining focused on the content that is being presented to you. The material that follows is practical but powerful, simplistic and yet solidified by its substance and straightforward suggestive points.

Do not skip this chapter because you feel that this does not apply to you; get the information so that you can check yourself and your marriage to be sure that there are no signs of vulnerability that you are overlooking because of overconfidence. Do not run away if you are a victim of infidelity. Stay right here at the table and eat this food with an open mind and allow it to bring health to your mind, body and spirit. Don't choke on conviction, just make the required changes, knowing that you can't change the past, but you can move forward into the future with information and insight that either you did not have or did not pay attention to in the past. Let's pray first:

> *Heavenly Father, You are so wonderful in Your person, so full of compassion and concern for Your children. Thank You for the love that You give unconditionally and without compromise. It is our prayer that as we unfold this information that You would cause our minds to open to the truth that is recorded here. Cause the innocent to be further enlightened concerning matters of infidelity, and the guilty to become transformed and repentant, knowing that You are able to give restoration to their fallen relationships. Holy Spirit, do not hide the truth from us, even if it hurts; just make us better for humanity so that we can live in the peace that the Father has for us. Amen.*

UNFULFILLED NEEDS

In chapter five, on the needs of men, we talked about how important it is to identify your needs with your mate with hope that those needs would be met. However, I want to go a little further on this subject because so many marriages today are threatened by the insensitivity of one partner toward the other one.

Having been in my profession for thirty years, I have had the opportunity of counseling many couples that have faced this issue. One of the most frequent complaints I hear from people who find themselves involved in relationships outside of their marriage is: "My spouse does not fulfill me anymore in areas where I have needs. I feel abandoned and rejected by my mate and feel as though I am not a priority." This is a very dangerous and vulnerable state of mind for a married person to be in, and if no attention is given, the unfulfilled spouse will begin seeking fulfillment elsewhere.

Despite the common perception, not all extra-marital relationships arise out of a need for sex. Most people assume that those who have affairs are looking for some extra sexual activity, but this is not always the case. And it definitely is not always so with the Spare Rib relationship. Sex is not always the source of an unfulfilled need, but it often becomes the payment given in return for the need that the Spare Rib has fulfilled.

The funny thing about needs is that people are willing to pay handsomely to have their needs met. This is why it is so important for couples to be open and honest with each other concerning their needs. It is the responsibility of marriage partners to identify with each other's needs and do all they can to accommodate and fulfill them. There will be some needs that a spouse will not be able to fulfill directly, but in those cases he or she must support the other partner indirectly for the filling of those needs, whatever they might be. Sometimes, meeting a mate's need does not require personal action or personal attention, just a proper and positive attitude that avoids provoking altercations.

The funny thing about needs is that people are willing to pay handsomely to have their needs met.

When we talk about the meeting of needs, we must be flexible in our assessment of them, because different people have different needs. Therefore, we must avoid stereotyping or a one-size-fits-all attitude when evaluating them. What works for one will not work for another, so we must not try to handle every need the same way. Needs are personal and custom-designed for each person, and, within certain general parameters, are as unique as the individuals they define. Any person in a relationship deserves to have his or her needs met. This is why it is so important for partners to share their needs with each other before marriage so that together they can establish a mutual support plan. The meeting of needs is not one-sided, but is the sharing of mutual responsibility, one for the other, with each taking ownership interest in the other's welfare, security, and happiness.

EMOTIONAL NEEDS

It is a common misconception that women are emotional but men are not. Men have feelings too, strong feelings, and often, but the expectations of society and survival in the dog-eat-dog world of the workplace have pressured men into adopting a mask of cool, calm stability that holds their feelings tightly on the inside. All of us have emotional needs that we must manage if we are single, but manage with support and help from our partner if we are married or in a serious relationship.

Because men and women are different in their emotions, both must give attention to the emotional needs of their partners. This is an area where you cannot play the guessing game. You must get to know your mate by asking questions concerning the support that he or she needs from you. Don't ever assume that you know your mate without question. We humans are constantly evolving and changing, and this is especially true in relationships, because we have another person to shape and be shaped by as we interact together.

According to the experts, our human psychological and physiological natures and needs change every ten years. What we needed at nineteen is a whole lot different than what we need at twenty-nine, or thirty-nine. I have discovered that, just as businesses perform regular analytical assessments of their affairs to make sure their companies remain relevant and competitive within their time, so must we give the same attention to the emotional changes and progress of our mates.

Asking questions and showing emotional interest will comfort and encourage your mate. Oftentimes we wait until there is an emotional blow up before we give attention to the fact that our mate has been facing some emotional challenges. There will be times when silence is the remedy or support your mate needs, but be very careful that your silence does not come off as negligence.

As I said before, some of your mate's emotional needs will not warrant a response from you, or your personal involvement. All that will be needed is your support. As we grow up, our needs go up. Just because we mature does not mean we become independent of our need for emotional support from our spouse. Sometimes it's not about tampering with your mate's emotional need as much as it is about pampering the need. Never forget that as long as you are connected to your mate, there will never cease to be a time when he or she will not need your support and your sensitivity. As a matter of fact, you should never want your mate to grow out of a need for you in any area. If that happens, what does it say about your relationship?

When you marry someone, you are saying to that person, "I have exercised all of my options, and you are it for me; therefore, I have no other options except you, as far as a mate is concerned." Always remember that whenever people have options, they can also exercise them whenever things get rocky. Our emotions are so changeable that we cannot afford to build a relationship solely upon them. Strive to be a source of support for each other, always making each other feel needed. Never assume that your mate does not have a particular need just because you do not have it. Remain focused on your mate, remembering always that emotions can be very fragile; so guard them with tender care.

> *Loving examinations are essential for loving expectations.*

Prevention is the best plan of protection as it relates to certain emotional breakdowns. Your plan should always be to provide such a base of communication with your spouse so that it becomes easy to detect when he or she is facing an emotional challenge. People who do not study each other will never reach each other. You must be suited to meet the needs of the person you are in relationship with. You should never expect a conflict to be resolved in your marriage if you do not know the emotional patterns and personalities of your mate. Loving examinations are essential for loving expectations. Stay alert, because emotions change constantly, and your mate will need your help through these emotional shifts.

Here is a poem for persuasive pampering:

I NEED YOU

I need you all of the time, not just in my body, but in my mind.

There are challenges that I face from day to day,

But when I have your support, I know that everything is OK.

Sometimes I really just need you to get inside of my head,

I promise, if you do, it would make things better in our bed.

Life can bring changes to your personality,

But when two people understand each other,

It doesn't change who they be.

I know that we've been together for a very long time,

And we both have emotional needs; you've got yours and I've got mine.

But when all has been said and done and the conversations are through,

I want you to always know that I will always need you.

SEXUAL NEEDS

The subject of sexual needs is so sensitive that many couples simply avoid any serious dialogue about it. This is due to many factors, not the least of which is the many differing opinions concerning what is right and wrong when it comes to sex between two persons. Because I have chosen to be open and real, I will not give you textbook opinions, but rather share my own personal views based on personal experience. My purpose is not to put forth my experiences as the standard, but simply to offer knowledge based upon experience as opposed to theoretical speculation.

The world we live in is very divided on the subject of sex. There is the religious view, the cultural view, the conservative view, the occult view, the biblical view, and the list goes on and on. Many marriages are held in bondage because of the divisive views that people have concerning sex. For this reason, I want to go straightforward at this subject.

When it comes to sex between a married couple, it is my view that nothing agreed upon between them is forbidden. It should be understood, of course, that this excludes any sexual activity that would extend beyond the two of them, such as threesomes, group sex, etc. Sex is a strong emotional expression of spouses' feelings toward each other. I do not believe there should be sexual restrictions, regulations, or rules when two persons are married and committed to each other. A confused or complex sexual life in a marriage can create a great deal of stress and struggle in that relationship. I strongly believe that a healthy sex life in a marriage is a major key to the life and tenure of that marriage.

No one marries and then expects to have rejection and boredom in their bedroom. The bedroom is the most sacred and special place in the home. It is there that dreams are realized, feelings are shared, love is expressed, visions are birthed, children are conceived, and passion is expressed. Because there are so many different views and opinions regarding sex, every couple must have open communication and honesty with respect to their sexual needs.

Since there is no set standard related to sex in marriage, each individual couple must set the standard that works for their particular relationship. This is an area where couples must be very clear and distinct about what they enjoy and do not enjoy. I recommend that couples take the time to explain their sexual perspective and needs to each other before they get married. This is not an area to spring surprises after the wedding. Express to your prospective partner honestly what it takes to fulfill your sexual appetite, and encourage him or her to do the same. If your prospective partner cannot accommodate your need, then perhaps he or she is not the right person for you. The last thing either of you want is to end up like many other marriages I know of where couples are not compatible sexually and resort to engaging in ungodly sexual scenarios outside of their marriages in order to find the sexual fulfillment they need.

Something is tragically wrong when a husband or wife has to look outside the marriage to find sexual fulfillment. The underlying cause usually is an incompatibility issue, a love issue, a lack of communication and understanding, or any combination of the three. Once your prospective mate reveals his or her sexual needs, and you agree to the marriage without objection, you obligate yourself to rise to the occasion whenever it comes. Otherwise, you will be guilty of deception in the first degree.

This leads me to another view on the subject of sex: sex as an obligation. I do not believe in "duty" sex, but rather, "desired" sex. I would not want to be intimate with my wife if I knew she was only doing it out of her marital responsibility. To me, a duty mentality in a relationship is not as relational as desire. I want my wife to want *me* as the source of her sexual fulfillment, not to just have sex with me for my sake. What's more, I would not want to feel that she was engaging in sex with me to keep me from straying. Most humans want to be desired and needed by their mate. Passion for your mate creates power and stamina to go the distance with an unselfish regard. Oftentimes it can also lead to positive competition to please each other, which can be very sensually and erotically entertaining.

> *Love is an unconditional emotion that is driven by its performance, not its reception.*

Making love to your mate is a sexual principle that both of the sexes need to learn, but especially men. There is a difference between when two people have sex and when they make love. In lovemaking, there is a connection of mind and spirit that happens before the two bodies even touch. When love for the other person is the driving force and pleasing him or her is the standard for having sex, there can be no disappointments or dissatisfaction.

The problem arises from the fact that we cannot make a person feel for us; they have to feel it in order to deliver it. Love is an unconditional emotion that is driven by its performance, not its reception. That's why, when I hear of these sexual problems in a marriage, I know right away that the persons in question are dealing with some things beneath the surface of the excuse they have given.

No man or woman who truly loves their spouse will be insensitive to the sexual needs of their spouse unless they have in some way lost their perspective concerning that person. Love between a husband and wife is expressed in their sexual relationship. God made man and woman to desire each other. People desire each other all of the time, but when they get married and after awhile stop having sex, or find their sex increasingly infrequent and unfulfilling, something is wrong.

Whatever the particular situation may be, an unfulfilled sex life is damaging to both marriage partners. Because every situation is different, just as every personality is different, it is impossible to prescribe one particular remedy that would suit everyone. I can tell you, however, that it is not normal behavior to be married and unwilling to meet the sexual needs of your mate. There are sex therapists and counselors who can assist you in this process. Look for one who will address your problem from the biblical perspective. Professional sex "therapy" from the ungodly perspective of the world may only make things worse.

Personally, I believe that the major key towards eliminating this problem is pre-counseling. If we would take preventive measures in the pre-counseling guidance process, we could eliminate most post-marital sexual problems. If you are planning to get married, seek professional and spiritual guidance from someone who will tell you the truth after giving you all of the facts. In the meantime, if you are facing a sexual crisis within your marriage, be assured that it doesn't mean that you have to divorce your mate; there is a way to make it through every crisis that comes your way as long as you are willing to face it and not run from it.

Do not listen to the negative voice in your ear that will lead you to believe that you are alone in this matter. Do not isolate yourself in shame or embarrassment, but insulate yourself by sharing your pain with those who love you and those whom you can trust. There are many persons just like you who have faced, and are still facing, the very same crisis as yours. Remain positive and know that nothing will ever change unless changes are made willingly.

In conclusion, when you are going through any crisis that involves another person, especially your spouse, it is important that you keep the lines of communication open at all times. Never go silent, because you could send a message that your spouse will interpret as insensitivity, which could open the door to infidelity. I would also recommend that the two of you spend some time together in prayer as well, always seeking God's guidance and help. Pamela, my wife of 27 years, and I, can guarantee you from our own experience that it will make a difference. Strive with much diligence to make your marriage a sexually enjoyable relationship for you and your mate. I cannot guarantee that this will keep your relationship from falling victim to the spare rib trap, but it will give your relationship a much better chance of survival than if you do not secure it sexually.

UNEXPRESSED FEELINGS — WHEN YOU DON'T SAY ANYTHING

One of the cancerous malignancies of a failing marital relationship is when two persons become so comfortable with each other that they neglect the importance of romantic and emotional expressions of their feelings toward each other. Many times we take for granted that our mate is aware of our feelings, and therefore no longer needs affirmation or reminding on a regular basis. On the contrary: we never outgrow our need to hear the person we love and who loves us to express those feelings frequently in words.

A common misconception holds that only women need to hear their men say that they love them; men don't need to hear it from their women. I completely disagree. I am a man, and it is highly important to me to hear my wife say that she loves me, not for confirmation, but rather, for consolation.

Verbal expression of feelings is a form of intimacy that can be very soothing and refreshing to a spouse, especially when he or she is confronted by other positive compliments from people outside the marriage. Here's an important tip: *"The expression of words creates effective communication that will help towards the elimination of excessive conflict."* Assuming that your mate does not need to hear your feelings of love expressed continually is a risky assumption that could lead your mate to conclude that you no longer care.

In many cases, couples respond to their mates based upon how they would like their mates to respond to them. This is perfectly fine as long as the needs of both partners are being met. Remember, opposites often attract, and if careful management is not given to the differences of needs between the two, someone in the relationship is going to be disappointed. As I said before, just because you don't need it, don't assume that your mate doesn't either. Relationships that are at risk are usually relationships that refuse to follow the principles of caring and sensitivity consciousness. Pay close attention to these matters, because if you do not, someone else will, and that someone else may very well steal away the affections of the one you love.

I want to encourage all couples, whether married or planning on marriage, to get out of yourselves long enough to get into your mates and make them the top priority of your attention. Many persons succeed in the business world, managing and giving oversight to major companies and developments; However when it comes to their mates, they can never manage to stop long enough to say, "I love you. You look good today. You smell good today. I missed you today," etc. But when it all comes crashing down, they discover that someone else has been buying their stock one share at a time, and, where once they were the sole stockholder, they are now the minority in a relationship they could have and should have managed much more wisely, and with heartfelt attention.

Pay attention to your relationship. Don't get out of the habit of expressing your feelings for your mate openly and verbally. It will pay lifelong dividends.

UNSECURED EGOS: "I WAS JUST TESTING THE WATERS TO SEE IF I STILL HAD IT."

Egocentricity is the philosophical idea of oneself without the consciousness that there exists anyone other than oneself. This naturally leads to a person becoming self-absorbed, self-assuming, self-ambitious, self-attentive and self-assertive. There are pros and cons to an egocentric nature that deserve fair assessment and treatment. It is not all bad to have a positive ego as long as you are mature enough to keep it under strong discipline. You must be careful and wise, however, to make sure that your ego does not lead you into a place of self-proving or self-competition. Our mind controls our emotions and desires; therefore, we must also have a spiritual and mental gallery of principles and standards that govern our flesh. If we have no such principles and standards, then we are subject to do anything and everything without regard for the feelings of other persons whose lives are affected by our actions.

Traditional belief says that only men have egos. This is absolutely false. Every human being, both male and female, has an ego; however, the manner in which those egos manifest themselves differ according to individual character and personality. I want to point out here that I am not addressing the issue of an insecure ego, but rather, an unsecured ego. This is the ego of a person who for some reason or another has not brought his or her need of being needed under control. Because the human ego thrives off the attention that it receives from others, whenever that attention is not given, the person with an unsecured ego will begin to search for other ways to feed it.

How does this affect those persons who are in committed relationships of marriage and others who are contemplating marriage? One of the things I have discovered about relationships with longevity is that many times a spirit of complacency, commonality and comfort forges its way into the fabric of good relationships, causing the persons within those relationships to lose attentive consciousness of each other due to familiarity. In most cases where infidelity (or the Spare Rib syndrome, as I call it) exists, it is in many cases due to the fact that many couples become so comfortable with each other that they forget to remain focused on the nature of the person they are in relationship with. Couples must always beware of the common ego-enticing temptations that are prone to come after them.

If one or the other partners in a marriage has an unsecured ego that has not matured past the feeling of needing to "retest the waters" to see if it can still turn a head or two, when there is a head at home, then that person is walking on dangerous ground. One thing I observed is that many know how they got out of the boat; they just don't know how they are going to get back in.

There are some areas of testing that married persons don't need to venture into. The safest place is the straightest place; keep yourself guarded against that ego and grounded in the truth regarding the propensity of your personality. Some people can't handle too many compliments without being thrown off track. If you are such a person, and you are married, you should have open conversations with your mate, related to your ego needs. If the two of you are not on the same page with regard to the fulfillment of those needs, then your marriage is vulnerable to the conceits of an unsecured ego, which could open the door to infidelity.

Despite legitimate ego needs, sometimes the unsecured ego *is* the problem, not one's mate. Whenever we do not walk in a spirit or manner of discipline, we are subject to give in to anything at anytime. I readily confess, without any regard to public criticism, that my ego has been the enemy in my life in many cases where I became distracted by the attention that I received in certain situations. I found myself lacking confidence that my wife was really into me at the level of my need, so that when people began to pay me special attention, I had a tendency to develop a dependence upon that kind of attention.

All of us love attention to one degree or another, but the unsecured ego lives for attention, and will in some cases break all the rules in order to feed the insatiable hunger of that psychological stronghold. If this sounds like you, then please give heed to this advice: talk to your partner and help him or her understand the importance of this need. And to your partner I would say, "Remember the commitment you made to your spouse. It was a total commitment that mandates you to cover him or her in every way. Don't neglect your mate's admission of need. Be willing to do everything necessary to keep him or her fulfilled."

So there it is. I do not claim to have all the answers, but I do know, without fear of contradiction, that if you apply the principles presented in this book, you will find it very easy to guard your marriage against the Spare Rib syndrome…and enter a marriage relationship that is richer, deeper and more fulfilling than you have ever imagined.

Commentary and Conclusion

It is with a humble spirit of anticipation that I hope your journey into *The Rib Connection* has proven to challenge you beyond your expectations, change you beyond your personal exposure, and charge you for better experiences in the future. It was my goal to be relevant, resourceful, and real as it relates to relationships. The joy of a relationship is often missed due to mismanagement and mediocrity. Through the philosophical principles and wisdom that I have been able to acquire through my years of experience, education, and spiritual enlightenment, *The Rib Connection* will definitely give you favorable results as you apply the information obtained to your relationship.

The beauty of a healthy relationship can be so fulfilling that a commitment to your mate becomes a normal response. It was through this book that I wanted all of its readers to arrive at a place in their lives where they understood the justification within their expectation. Whenever you are willing to commit yourself to an individual for a lifetime, you have the right to expect the best of everything from within that relationship. It is again my hope that you have found some explosive insights that will cause you to never compromise the high standards that you should strive for as you endeavor to be connected to a life-lasting relationship.

May the hope of God who gives both strength and life keep you as you experience everything that He has purposed for your life.

Carlos L. Malone, Sr.

Bishop Carlos Malone, Sr.

—————————————

Bishop Carlos Malone, Sr. is the Senior Pastor/Teacher of Bethel Full Gospel Baptist Church, a thriving and diverse ministry located in the Richmond Heights community of Miami, Florida.

Bishop Malone has been anointed to minister the Word of God for more than two decades. He has become world renowned for his charismatic gift to deliver the Word with a "no-holds-barred" approach without compromising, falsifying, or watering down the true essence of the Bible.

He has touched an abundance of lives across the globe through his dynamic and prophetic preaching and teaching, emphasizing personal empowerment and church growth.

In addition to preaching and teaching, he has been anointed with a unique gift of song, bringing him worldwide recognition as a "tenor extraordinaire." He has been featured on several recordings, including *Bethel In Praise*; *O' Come Let Us Adore Him*; and Full Gospel Baptist Church Fellowship International's first CD release entitled *A New Thing*, also featuring the talents of Bishop Paul Morton, Be-Be Winans, Byron Cage, and a host of other artists. In 2004, Bishop Malone released his solo debut CD entitled *Thirst No More*. He recently recorded his sophomore project, *Enter In*, which is scheduled for release this year. Bishop Malone has also produced and directed theatrical works, which include *Jesus For The People* and *O' Come Let Us Adore Him.*

Bishop Malone has authored several other books, including *The Integrity of Ministry, God's Created Order, and Hidden In His Hands.*

Bishop Malone is an extraordinary man with an extraordinary gift, striving to do extraordinary things to bring people closer to God by enlightening them about the Power, Principles, and Promises revealed in the Word of God.

He is a devoted husband to his wife Pamela, who is his partner in ministry, and a loving father to his children——twin daughters Ashley and Andrea and son Carlos, Jr., and his beloved godson Raymond Young.

The heart of Bishop Malone as he approaches his 50th birthday celebration in November of this year is to be *reachable, relevant, and radical* in reaching the world for our Lord. His focus is to provide people with an avenue by which they can come to know God.

www.TheRibConnection.com